The
Astonishing History of Newport

A History of a Shropshire Market Town

Malcolm Miles

2010

Published by Malcolm Miles

The Birches, Avenue Road South, Newport, Shropshire. TF10 7DY.

E-mail susanmiles.newport@virgin.net

First published 2010.

ISBN. 978-0-9548531-3-6

Printed and bound in Great Britain by: W.M. Print Limited
Registered office:
45-47 Frederick Street, Walsall, West Midlands, WS2 9NE.

Contents

Foreword

This is a collection of essays on the more unusual people and events in Newport's history.

Somebody, somewhere, once wrote that the shortest story ever was one line that went like this: "My god the Duchess is pregnant, who did it." This it is said includes all the basics for a good story - religion, sex, class and mystery. Well this short book intends to go further adding fraud, bigamy, greed, snobbery, seduction, sadism and terrorism all within one small, rural town. It records the decline and fall - like Rome - of institutions and a society once regarded as immutable.

We begin in the 1850`s with Mr Arthy at a time when Newport was settling into Victorian respectability and affluence. Was he a veterinary surgeon and a bigamist? He was certainly a thief. Was he unlucky or a rogue?

Harper Adams and his brother Joseph are renowned for their philanthropy in founding the Agricultural University at Edgmond, Shropshire. But what were their real motives, we suggest greed, hatred and snobbery and that they created something good out of their unnatural instincts.

The flight of the Irish after the famine of 1845 is an international story but their arrival in Newport had a profound effect on the town. Sad and shocking at first, they settled and became a welcome part of the community.

Fire though spectacular and exciting is a nasty business and if the methods of tackling it look hilarious it was a constant danger and only really tackled with the advent of war.

Duchess Blair insinuated herself into, and exploited, aristocratic society, exposing its nastier aspects. A sensation at the time, proof that sleaze has never gone away.

Poor Millicent Howle was seduced by a gentleman bounder as many had been before, leading to the humiliation of a group of aspiring middle class families in a small rural community.

The sadistic side of early education aimed at bringing learning to the lower classes is revealed in two cases of beatings or as they were more aptly described "floggings". But why was one caning found perfectly acceptable and the other punished? William Carr in "The Marked Man", and Walter Samuel Brooks in "Town Verses Gown" are exposed and compared.

The discovery of a photograph of an ornate wedding cake of 1909 leads to the tale of a funeral and four weddings and the end of a social group who once set the tone of the town.

In three generations the landed estates surrounding Newport disappeared. Some reasons are obvious but others not as straightforward as you would think.

Multiple murder in a quiet backwater of the second world war when victory was in sight, but was the motive as obvious as it looks?

For six hundred years the Newport May Fair stood in the High Street, in 1939 it ended and with it went the last link with Newport's Medieval past.

Tuckers is a building which had a great fall and all the Queen`s men could not put it together again!

For a small town to lose so much in such a short time was scandalous but was it inevitable or were there more sinister reasons. Take the case of Newport Cottage Hospital ……

The age of the IRA was frightening and unpleasant but was its connection with Newport coincidental or more pivotal?

We end with a strange, humorous but very patriotic footnote, all about a shoe.

What Happened To The Vet?

Frederick Henry Arthy came to Newport in September 1855, for the next month, 10 November 1855, we find a notice in the Newport Advertiser from Mr C Matthews, veterinary surgeon, recommending to his employers and the public generally, Mr F Arthy, veterinary surgeon, MRVCL, as his assistant. An assistant to a veterinary surgeon in the golden age of farming in the eighteen fifties and sixties was the right job to be in both financially and socially. Charles Matthews had been a respected vet in Newport, at Rosemont in Chetwynd End, then St Marys Street, for over twenty years but later became afflicted with paralysis and came to entrust the management of his business to his assistant. Frederick Arthy was a popular man his great grandchildren maintaining he was a charmer and certainly he was a sportsman and man about town for in February 1856, for example, we find him winning a pig shooting competition at the Fox and Duck, Pave Lane, a frequent pastime where groups of gentlemen would pay a fee, the winner taking the pig and everyone would enjoy a meal and convivial evening afterwards.

However in July 1858 Arthy appeared at the Newport Petty Sessions in front of the magistrate Sir T.F.F.Boughey of Aqualate Park charged with forgery. The court was crowded during the hearing of the cases, for there were several charges, because, as we have seen, the prisoner was well known and respected in Newport and the neighbourhood and the affair "....had cast a sad gloom among his immediate friends...." What had he been up to in this position of trust? Firstly in February 1858 he forged an acceptance and receipt for £7.16.06 (£7.82) off George Paddock trading as Messrs John, George and William Paddock millers, at Caynton, with intent to defraud Matthews. Suzannah Matthews, wife of Charles, said she had given Arthy the money and he had brought the bill back as paid. George Paddock said the prisoner had never paid him any money nor had he given a receipt for the bill which was for flour supplied to Mr Matthews. The prisoner made no defence and was committed for trial.

There were two other charges for forgery for amounts of £3.07.00 (£3.35) and £3.09.00 (£3.45) on acceptance and receipt of Mr James Pidgeon assistant to William Liddle, wine merchant at the Vine Vaults, and Mr George Barlow, innkeeper at the Plume of Feathers. Again he made no defence and was committed.

The prisoner was then charged with having embezzled the sum of £3 and upwards on 15 January 1858 in the parish of Edgmond, the property of his master. James Paddock, junior, Chetwynd Aston, proved that the prisoner brought his father a bill amounting to £3.06.06 (£3.32) which his father at once paid. Suzannah Matthews said that the name of Paddock appeared in her ledger as a debtor because the prisoner said the amount had not been paid. She had never received any part of that bill nor had Arthy accounted for it. Mr Matthew`s brother gave similar evidence. A second charge of embezzlement was for having received £4.09.09 (£4.49) off Mr John Icke, a farmer of Cheswell, which he had not paid over or accounted for. Both these were proved and he was committed.

Arthy, aged 36, was stood at the bar at Shropshire Summer Assizes at the end of July 1858 charged on four counts of embezzlement from Mr Matthews. He intended to plead not guilty but was persuaded in his own interests to change this to guilty. He was brought up again a few days later and sentenced to three years penal servitude.

The loss was so great and so much sympathy felt for Mr Matthews over the conduct of his assistant that a subscription was raised in September 1858 by a committee of several eminent local people, these included the Rev.W Elliot of Chetwynd Rectory; Messrs Holland and Son, estate agents in St Marys Street, Newport; Mr Cobb, architect and builder, Chetwynd End; Messrs Jones and Aston, ironmongers, Lower Bar; Mr Asterley, Adeney; Mr William Paddock, Old Caynton; Mr William Challinor, Ellerton Mill; Mr John Bullock, Donnington Wood Mill; Mr Stokes, Pilson Hill; Mr Machin, Cowley; Mr Joseph Booker, Weston Jones Mill and Mr Belcher, Moreton. A subscription list in the Advertiser has over 52 names and these were the ones donating over 2/6 (25p) such as Holland and Son £2, T.H.Burne £5, local solicitors, Heane, Fisher and Liddle and the Rector and master at the Grammar School. Over £82 was raised, it was truly a large, local scandal. Matthews retired that month through ill health after 35 years in business and was replaced by R.G.Walters of Eccleshall. He died in February 1864 aged 70, at Pave Lane.

Arthy was back in Newport in 1861 lodging at the Barley Mow describing himself as unmarried, aged 38, (ie born 1823), a veterinary surgeon from Colchester in Essex. But what was he doing back in town so soon? Had he served his three years? Was he unmarried? Was he a vet?

Frederick Arthy appears in the 1841 census in the parish of Earls Colne, Essex aged 25 (ie born 1816), a veterinary surgeon, along with his wife Eliza aged 20 also of Essex. This is the only record of Eliza Barnes though there were two children of the marriage, Charles Arthy registered in March 1841 and Susanna Barnes Arthy registered March 1845. The children were brought up by their grandmother Bridget Barnes who in 1851 was widowed and living at Colne Green, Earls Colne, Essex with the children and her 25 year old son Robert. She was listed as a gardener and he as a gardener's assistant. Susanna died aged 12 which would be about 1857 the time her father was embezzling. His son Charles became a carpenter and had a son Frederick C Arthy, an ironfounders clerk, and in 1901 Charles, listed as a widower, is living with Frederick, his wife and four children, at Park Lane, Earls Colne in Essex. So Frederick Arthy of Newport had a son and grandchildren.

Just to the east of Colchester are the villages of Stanway and Fordham and here were to be found many Arthys who by 1900 had spread as far as Australia and California some still veterinary surgeons. Whites Directory of Essex in 1845 has Henry Bentley Arthy at the Post Office at Stanway and in 1851, aged 30, he is listed as born in nearby Fordham and is a veterinary surgeon, a licensed victualler at the Swan Inn and the Post Office, Stanton. There were two daughters 8 and 3 both born in Stanway. In 1861 now suddenly aged 47, he is in Stanway Street as a Veterinary surgeon.

Frederick's brother, Charles Arthy was born in 1818 and was Relieving Officer and Registrar of Births and Deaths at Fordham in 1881. It was Charles' son William Henry Arthy who joined his uncle in Newport as a veterinary surgeon though in 1871 aged 18 he was a drapers' assistant. Where and when did he qualify as a vet?

In February 1864 Frederick Arthy married Annie Bradbury at St Mary's in Shrewsbury with only the Parish Clerk and his wife as witnesses. Why was this when there were several sisters, and her parents were stalwarts of the village of High Offley, for generations being owners of the Royal Oak the local inn near the church. This was because it was a runaway marriage and though he described himself at the ceremony as a "bachelor" he certainly had had a wife and family when he left Essex around 1850. Not only was it a bigamous marriage but he was seventeen years older than her, she was 28 and he frequently lied about his age right up to his death.

James Bradbury born c.1796 was the landlord of the Royal Oak at High Offley, for fifty years combining this, along with his two sons, with the trade of builder and bricklayer. He had three daughters, Mary who married John Wakefield, Ann or Annie who married Frederick Arthy and Ellen who became Mrs Hartley. The pub rests under the bank of the church where the Bradleys lie buried together. Charles Bradbury also came from High Offley and in 1841 aged 20 was a tailor's apprentice married to Sarah Smart the daughter of his master, James Smart. He remained a tailor and draper in the High Street, Newport, until he took over the Royal Oak in the 1870's. His daughters married local tradespeople, Norris', watchmakers and Cartwrights', tobacconists. Anne Arthy was part of an extended local family.

In November of that year, newly married, Arthy moved to Prospect Place, a house so called because it had views right down the High Street to the market place. On the corner of Wellington Road it is now (2010) an empty plot with a seat and flower bed but was once an imposing house. It had for a while been a school for young ladies run by Helen Bradbury. The school moved and Arthy took over renaming the building the "Veterinary Infirmary", animal bones found when the building was demolished proving this usage.

WELLINGTON ROAD CORNER, NEWPORT.
PERFECTION SERIES 1304.

Prospect Place on left

Arthy was bankrupt by January 1867 though his release was opposed on the suspicion that he had a large income which he had not revealed, so proceedings were adjourned for payments and receipts to be produced which showed debts of £163. They stayed on the corner of Wellington Road until August 1869 when his household goods including his pony and trap were sold up. During this period of bankruptcy two of his little boys died and are buried in High Offley churchyard.

High Offley Church.

At the 1871 census mother and father and two daughters aged three and eleven months had moved in with Mrs Arthy's sister at what is now 72 Upper Bar. Mary had also been born at High Offley and was the wife of John Wakefield a horsebreaker and clipper who had been the last tenant of the White Horse a pub demolished in 1860 to build the market hall. It must have been crowded as the Wakefields had six children. His son James Bradley Arthy died here aged 1year and nine months in February 1872 and a daughter, Florence, aged one year and ten months in December 1878.

All the time Frederick Arthy was describing himself as a veterinary surgeon and though his brother was a vet, and his nephew, and though he is listed as a veterinary surgeon in the 1868 edition of Slater's Directory of Shropshire and North Wales, there is no trace of him in the archives of the Royal College in London. Was he ever qualified or was he struck off over the 1858 case or the bankruptcy?

In December 1873 he was actually taking a man to court for non-payment of £1.19.00 (£1.95) over treatment of cattle. There is also evidence that he was doing work for the Duke of Sutherland on the Lilleshall Estate though this is likely to have been on a call-out, emergency basis.

A public notice in August 1880 thanks his friends for their patronage of thirty years suggesting that he must have been in Newport since 1850. He also announced that he had taken into partnership his nephew W.H.Arthy and that they would trade as F.H. and W.H.Arthy, veterinary surgeons, Upper Bar, Newport. By February 1881 they had moved to premises adjoining Mr Weales timber yard in Station Road. The census of that year has Arthy aged 57 (he was in fact 62) from Fordham in Essex, his wife Annie aged 45 from High Offley and four daughters, Ellen 16, Annie Marie 13, Ritornella 7 and Mary 6; William Henry Arthy, the nephew lodged with them aged 28, unmarried, a veterinary surgeon from Halstead in Essex. Despite all their financial troubles they had a female servant.

Within ten months the partnership had dissolved and W.H.Arthy set up in Gnosall. Frederick Arthy went into liquidation by arrangement in May 1882 still describing himself as MRCVS, and died in December aged 63.

Who exactly was this man? Family tradition has him as a greatly respected member of Newport society, not only a vet but a composer and church organist, but as more evidence turns up those who thought there was a skeleton in the cupboard are feeling justified, a charming rascal? a bit wild? probably both. A forger, convicted embezzler, bigamist, bankrupt, fake, but a family man, sociable, charming and a survivor.

Mrs Arthy certainly settled down into respectability living at Station Terrace and appearing under "Private Resident" in the local directories. The girls quickly married, Nellie, the elder, aged 20 in 1885, to Mr C Martin of Whitchurch who was employed by the London and North Western Railway Company; Mary (Polly), the youngest one aged 20, to William Alex Walker, Eccleshall, Staffordshire in 1893; Ritornelli (Rittie) in 1898 aged 24 to Mr C.A. Roberts of Tewksbury. All married at St Andrews Church, Church Aston. Annie (Nancy) had a private school in Newport from the 1880's and is listed as "School teacher" in 1891. She is also quoted in Station Road in 1899. She married Anthony Linden Covington in 1902. In 1901 Annie Arthy (Bradbury) is living with her daughter Ellen in New Brighton.

From this point the family disappear from Newport and the story of an intriguing character went with them.

The Adams Family.

In September 1901 after a luncheon provided by the Royal Victoria Hotel, guests adjourned to a large marquee for the public function the formal opening of the Harper Adams Agricultural College. The company included the Earl and Countess of Bradford, Lord and Lady Hatherton, Sir Thomas and Lady Boughey and The Right Hon. R.W.Hanbury. M.P., President of the Board of Agriculture. In a speech opening the College Mr Hanbury briefly acknowledged the founder, briefly because little was known about him and what was, was not very complimentary. Mr Harper Adams, he said, was a man who gave a large sum of money because he felt that agriculture sadly needed help. This was the way we supported great institutions in this country through private munificence rather than State interference. He then moved on to devote his speech to his main purpose to push for more State interference through central and local government by protection from foreign competition by putting more money into rural education to keep young people on the land instead of making them sick of country life. Model farms and agricultural shows were a waste of money he said, it was land agents who wanted educating and bailiffs who needed to be taught to add up. He had obviously forgotten, or did not know, that Sir Thomas Boughey had recently founded the Newport Agricultural Society with its annual show!

HARPER ADAMS AGRICULTURAL COLLEGE, EDGMO
PERFECTION SERIES 1742.

What we now know is that it is doubtful whether Thomas Harper Adams had such fine sentiments or profound thoughts about farming when he drew up his will. They do not tie in with his known character or history and were a shock to the gentlemen he selected to carry out his wishes.

Clause 7 of the will drawn up 28 October 1891 empowered his executors to apply the residue of his estate, after certain other small bequests, for the purpose of teaching practical and theoretical agriculture to men and youths, and a knowledge of dairying, housekeeping and other subjects to women and girls "which will tend to make them practical women in their station of life in England", either by means of lectures or by establishing a school or schools of agriculture at Edgmond or Woodseaves, near Market Drayton in the county of Salop, or at Chadwell in the county of Stafford, a former estate of his brother Joseph Harrison Adams. They were given discretion to choose any other place or places or other methods of applying the money to those ends. Though earlier wills had varied in detail this clause is the definitive one.

If you are looking for some logical philanthropic impulse behind his decision then it can be done and the official history of the College does this. It attempts to show a progression of thought to the conclusion of a College with Adams seeking advice, usually on the sly, and honing his ideas. It paints a picture of appalling agriculture decline in the 1890's with landowners like Sir Thomas Boughey cutting rents by 10 or even 20% and trying to revive enterprise by founding agricultural societies to encourage innovation. It shows the beginnings of agricultural education through the new (1888) County Councils though money was meagre and interest often desultory. Nevertheless Adams must have been aware of such efforts. Did these influence him?

There was no doubt about the money, the Adams family had spent more than a century building up land and property and safeguarding it to the detriment of most ordinary social attributes such as family, children, marriage, affection, neighbourliness and community feeling. On his death the wildest rumours prevailed because nobody knew, was it £100,000 or the £20,000 indicated in the will? C.R.Liddle the solicitor of the estate wrote to the County Council intimating that £50,000 would be available and inviting them to submit a trustee. Perhaps here is a clue, Liddle and certainly his son Roland Pemberton Liddle who quickly took over from his father, were social animals with social skills and social aspirations already administering local estates particularly Aqualate and

Sir Thomas Boughey. What a coup for the Liddles, what prestige in setting up a national institution based on the wealth of a miser who could not even sign his name. How clever to suggest Sir Thomas Boughey, S.T.H Burne and C.C.Cotes as trustees, people Harper Adams could not socialise with in life would now flatter him by association in death. Harper Adams and his brother had always had a fawning admiration for the upper classes even planning at one time to leave their wealth to the Anson family, the Lichfield's of Shugborough, nobility with whom they claimed some connection. The shock, horror, of these landed gentry when they realised the task they had been allotted and the status of the one who had bequeathed it is all too apparent.

Yet Liddle was to repeat the exercise in 1906 when on the death of Sir Thomas Boughey he was to use money from the estate to set up the Boughey Trust an institution he ran until his death in 1959. He was incidentally Clerk to Harper Adams College for fifty years.

But there are other reasons that suggest ulterior motives for the will, they are at best stubbornness at worst revenge. After all Harpers nearest, if not dearest, his wife Sarah Adams was a cousin and marriage was always a tool to secure property and ring fence it, and she was provided for with her own wealth and in the will all the horses, cows, pigs, poultry and "my household stores and six tons of hay if the same be standing on land in my occupation at my death absolutely", and the enjoyment of Edgmond House, buildings, land, furniture, carriage and harness, though she was to pay all taxes, rates and outgoings.

By leaving his wealth to the College no other relative would inherit and any counter claim would entail the odium of challenging a generous, public bequest. To understand this we have to look at the way Harper Adams acquired his money. This accrual of property may have been small time and some of the methods such as marriage to cousins and even half-sisters and manipulation of wills, distasteful, but eventually it meant a sizeable fortune in the hands of one man. The strands go back to the Adams family of Tibberton in the early 1700's and the Harper family at Stanton upon Hine Heath and Woodseaves. We will discount the fanciful connection with the Adams's of Sambrook and eventually the Lichfields. Nevertheless on a local level they were substantial property owners and apparently immune from the troughs and peaks of the agricultural world. The Ancellor Estate deeds show that in 1779 William Adams the younger purchased the estate from the Pigot family including the manors of

Edgmond, Chetwynd and Adeney; lands in Edgmond, Chetwynd, Newport, Longford, Drayton in Hales, Bedstone, Bucknell and Clungunford. The key date is 1804 when John Adams of Ancellor House married Sarah Harper. He was only 22. They had four sons William 1805-1835, John 1808-1831, Joseph Harrison 1813-1889 and Thomas Harper Adams 1817-1892.

In 1832 John made settlements on the three surviving sons, the Ancellor estate to William, the Chatwell portion to Joseph and land in Edgmond to Thomas who was to receive the Woodseaves estate from his uncle Harper. On the death of William, Harper Adams got the bulk of his brother's property. The land was being consolidated in fewer hands and with two brothers left how could that be furthered?

Ancellor House

Who was Harper Adams? With two brothers who kept to themselves there was plenty of gossip maturing into country legend. They were not the only eccentrics in the countryside and amongst the local gentry the Burton Boroughs on the neighbouring Chetwynd estate had similar traits, somewhat reclusive, one riding a penny farthing with an oilcan in his pocket shouting at those in his way, counting his fish and shooting his deer with a bow and arrow, spending much of his time in his workshops; his son, the last squire, more sociable, but still known as "barbed wire Jack" because of his tattered clothes, attending funerals in shorts and the magistrates court on a bicycle with his coat held up by binder twine.

Unkempt, unsociable, squeaky voiced, Harper was an obvious source of fun to local children as he travelled the lanes in his horse and cart but other such figures were at least lovable, Harper Adams was not. His miserliness led him to hate not only his family but the community and this was returned as dislike, fear and contempt. There was in this also the age old rural fear of the odd, the inexplicable, the residue of folklore and haunting images repeated around fires on dark nights in cottages and inns.

This view of his character is confirmed by a most unlikely source. By the 1890's the local newspaper was a Victorian institution and the Newport Advertiser owned and edited by a local liberal and nonconformist family was far removed from any taint of prejudice, superstition and ignorance. The death of any one of standing was always heralded by the newspaper as "casting a gloom" over the community and the editor was able to find redeeming features for the obituary of the lowest and the meanest reprobate. Yet this is his judgement on Thomas Harper Adams.

"When away from home we read our Advertiser last week and saw in the obituary the name of Thomas Harper Adams we confess the announcement did not stir us to any deep emotion. To say that Mr Adams had not made himself a popular man would be to put it in the mildest form. For years back he and his late brother too, the late John [sic: Joseph] Harrison Adams of Newport, appeared to cut themselves off from sympathy with almost all their neighbours and from the sphere of public movements which is expected of men in their position. Not only did they fail to inaugurate any schemes for the general good but their names were conspicuously absent from subscription lists and as little was expected of their private charity. It was therefore with surprise amounting to incredulity that people heard of Mr Adams's munificent bequest to the public." [Newport Advertiser. 18 June 1892] In a report a week later the newspaper condemns his wealth as "ill gotten gains".

Other reasons for his behaviour really only refer to the last years of his life. One was interbreeding, the other illness, probably stemming from the former. Interbreeding was familiar in English economic and social

11

life and was the result of class, lack of travel and choice and the need for a family to cushion its long term security with property and land. Interbreeding, even incest, were common to all classes and Laurie Lee refers to it up lonely, isolated country roads in Gloucestershire. Adams was very ill, perhaps paranoiac, at the end, but it is hard to argue that these two factors focussed his benevolent, public side, nor was it due to madness as suggested by the defendants in the will case. Longer term fixations determined his bequest.

The sale of the property and the realisation of the funds to build the College had to wait a year until 1893 after the settlement of legal disputes. There were two sales the first dealing with property and land and the other personal effects. The second sale was over five days as was that of his brother three years earlier and shows a remarkable accumulation of objects for a country farmer again similar to his brother Joseph. The sale on July 1 - 4 and July 7 had on day one books, paintings and engravings; day two antiques, silver, pottery and china; day three antique furniture, oak carvings, glass and wine; day four bedroom furniture, bedsteads, cabinets, dining room furniture, arms and armour; day five bed and table linen, kitchen and domestic offices, outdoor effects, horses and carriages and 60 tons of hay. The property sale included land in Woodseaves, Edgmond, Littlehales and Chadwell the latter being the former estate of his brother Joseph. There were eleven lots in Newport, again probably from his brother and the Blakemore estate, two cottages in Wellington Road and the Hare Meadow or Town Meadow at one time the cricket field and now the Girls High School; there were two cottages in Beaumaris Road and a field, and on the High Street the shops of Messrs Lunn, printers, Brown, china, Griffiths and Son, painters and plumbers and three cottages. Also sold were 25 shares in Newport Market Company nominal value £20 each.

The Chadwell estate, property in Newport and some of the household items came from his brother Joseph Harrison Adams who was the third son and four years older then Harper. A sister Sarah died a baby in 1822. Joseph came to live at Adams House in High Street, Newport its Georgian façade hiding a much older building. John Adams was living there in 1797 and Jane Adams until 1836. Joseph Adams married that year and this could be because he had come into possession of the house, he is certainly there in 1841 when his daughter was aged three. This was, and is, a substantial house when sold in 1926 by H Kilvert-Minor-Adams consisting of entrance hall, sitting room, dining room, kitchen and pantry;

on the first floor a drawing room, two bedrooms and offices; second floor two bedrooms and two attics. Outside there was a coach house, gardens, a large malthouse, another coach house and stables, cow houses, saddle and cart rooms. There were two fields of pasture, 6.5 acres, and two more fields up the Wellington Road. A comfortable dwelling lived in by Joseph until his death in 1889, without necessity of earning a living. In 1851 he described himself as landed proprietor and commissioner of taxes.

Adams House

On 19 April 1836 Joseph, then at Sheriffhales married Mary Anne Blakemore witnesses being Robert George Higgins, a Newport surgeon, Sarah Smith and Mary Blakemore. He was 23 and she 41. How and why they married given the age difference we do not know but that the families knew each other and did business together is shown by an account from Blakemore's to the executors of John Adams for funeral materials made out for 11 June 1832 the day John Adams died. Joseph had a landed name, was minor gentry, with an imposing town house. Mary Anne brought a substantial commercial income to the union.

The 1832 billhead shows Blakemore's on the site of the present library on the High Street, the castellated shop there then as now. The business was

T Blakemore junior and Co, linen and woollen drapers, importers of silks, Irish linen, French Cambries, long lawns, furs, parasols, carpets, leghorn and straw bonnets and providers of a complete funeral service. In 1831 Thomas Blakemore senior is quoted as having a large warehouse in Bakehouse Lane, Stafford Street, used for woolstapling, and a messuage between the Red Lion and his own house, now the site of a library. He had purchased this as a malthouse and converted it into a mercers and drapers shop erecting a gasometer and gas house for the production of gas for the newly erected shop. This was four years before the town gasworks opened. That same year Thomas Blakemore junior and Mary Anne dissolved their partnership as mercers, drapers and woolstaplers and by 1835 and 1836 she is listed under "Gentry". The family were also in to malting and banking. Mary Anne, E.A.Blakemore and John Blakemore were shareholders in Blakemores Bank and Thomas was manager though not a shareholder. They were part of the Commercial Bank, Birmingham, which had at least seventeen branches from Liverpool and Manchester to Ludlow. The bank failed in 1840 and Thomas Blakemore moved on to the National Provincial Bank keeping his drapery business until April 1846 when he sold out to John Warner for £3,100.

One reason why the bank failed was a famous theft of the bank box containing £1,700 from the Holyhead mail coach between Shifnal and Birmingham on the Saturday night, 22 December, 1838. Most of the money was in bills of exchange, cheques and drafts which were stopped; £35.75 was in silver coin.

Mary Anne therefore brought a considerable amount to the marriage estimated in the 1893 will case at £15,000 which on her death in May 1856 aged 61 went to her husband which under the law of the time was his anyway unless a marriage settlement had been made beforehand. Joseph was still only 42 and his daughter, Mary Anne Blakemore Adams, 18. On 22 January 1858 he drew up a will in which he "gave, devised and bequeathed all his real and personal estate to his brother Thomas Harper Adams of Edgmond in the County of Salop, gentleman, absolutely and appointed him his sole executor." In 1863 Thomas drew up a similar will in favour of his brother a kind of tontine, a life insurance increasing as each subscriber dies. It came into effect when Joseph died in June 1892. His daughter blamed her uncle Thomas`s influence for the will and her later rejection and lack of financial help from her father, but in 1892 the newspaper repeated the long held local belief that the will was a mutual affair by the two brothers. "A report gained currency years ago that the two brothers Mr J.H.Adams and Mr T.H.Adams had agreed that the survivor of them should inherit all the property and that he should leave it to a certain noble family with which he believed the Adams`s claim some connection."

In 1858 Joseph was not the puppet and recluse some would make out, he was a Trustee under the new Marsh Act of 1854 and we find him in dispute with them over his attempts to enclose the land in front of Adams House out of the highway. In 1858 he was a shareholder in the newly formed Market Company which built the market hall and livestock market, and with 15 shares worth £300 he had a substantial investment which entitled him to become a director. He was also a JP for Staffordshire through his Chatwell estate. Certainly as time went on he withdrew from these interests but in 1858 he must have known what he was doing.

Mary Anne Blakemore Adams, the daughter, married in 1862 John Minor a farmer from Tern Hill then Shrewsbury and Wem, this was after the grand decision made in the two wills. Her decision to marry someone they considered beneath her and rather worthless in business therefore did not influence the decision though they used the marriage to justify it. The lack of money of the couple was due, according to the brothers, to the dissipation of the husband and help was continually refused, attempts at reconciliation rejected and correspondence unanswered. The marriage of John Minor and Miss Adams was reported in the Newport Advertiser of 14 June 1862 and there was no doubt where the sympathies of the editor and the townsfolk lay. Uncertainty as to when the wedding would be meant that tokens were not so numerous even so the church and the streets were decorated. The bride was given away by the Rev. Sandford, minister at Newport and second master at the Grammar School. The wedding was at 9 am followed by dejeuner at the Royal Victoria Hotel and the bridal pair emerged to hearty hurrahs testifying to the respect and esteem of the town. She was, said the newspaper, a young lady of gentle and amiable disposition whose attributes and kindness had won the affection of everyone and they hoped all her best wishes would be realised. This deliberate enthusiasm emphasised the meanness and dislike of her father and uncle Harper who of course were not at the wedding.

Consequently on the death of Joseph Harrison Adams in September 1889 the estate went to his brother. The Advertiser reported "On Monday morning last the town was surprised to hear that Mr Adams was dead. He

15

had been seen to the very end of the week and as late as 7 o'clock on Saturday evening he was with the gardener in his garden. At a later hour he felt ill and remained in bed on Sunday and before dawn on Sunday he expired. The deceased gentleman was a Justice of the Peace for Staffordshire though for many years he took no active part in magisterial work. He was the owner of a nice landed property at Chatwell and of considerable house property in Newport. In accordance with his express wish application was made to open the family vault in Newport church but the Home Secretary declined to give consent." The churchyard had been closed since 1858. The 1890 rate assessment shows him with house, land, malthouse, thirteen cottages, gardens and three other houses empty. By this time he was living in that huge house with one servant.

The unreserved sale of the contents of Adams House in June 1890 revealed an amazing secreted hoard. The Advertiser understated when it said "it is well known that for many years Mr Adam's house had been as full as a museum." This is just a shortened list of the five day sale: a unique collection of old furniture, carvings, china, books, coins, silver plate and bric a brac; a grand Elizabethan oak bedstead, chests, cabinets and carvings; old black-lettered books of the earliest editions, County histories, pictures and engravings; buhl [form of inlay] and marqueterie cabinets and chairs; old oriental, English and other china; arms and armour; household furniture, carriages and horses. Mr T.W.Picken writing in 1891 maintained that Joseph Adams had in his house an old, carved piece of oak from the pulpit of Lichfield Cathedral and six oak panels in his dining room, 3 feet by 11 inches, of saints, inscribed 1602 also from Lichfield.

Mrs Minor immediately contested the wills and won an annuity of £200 which was taken into account in the final settlement in 1893. She accepted this as no one had a clue what the estate was worth. The Advertiser in June 1892 had no idea either: "the neighbourhood had become so accustomed to consider Mr Thomas Adams as a person from whom nothing was to be expected that we never heard a speculation or a guess at the manner in which his large wealth would be disposed of ...the sum available is reckoned from £100,000 to £150,000 ...Thomas Harper has been an invalid laid up with an incurable disease and knowing that the only question was when the end would come. He must have often pondered what he should do with his wealth. We should suppose it would frequently be his chief occupation."

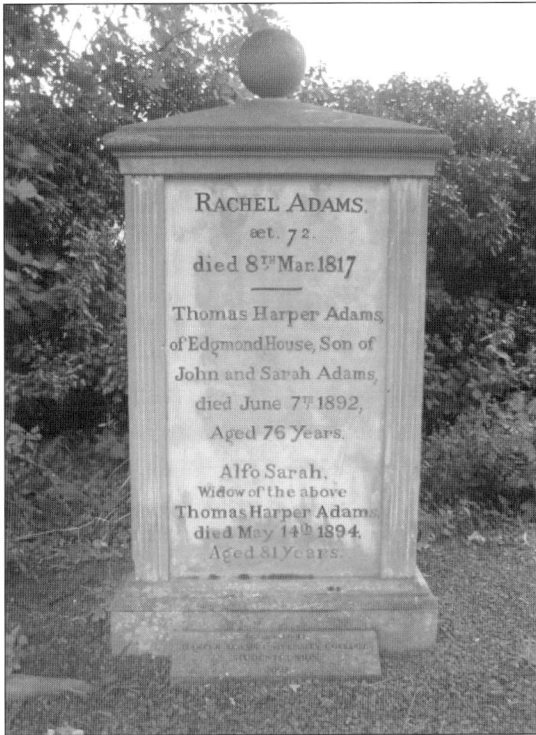

Adams family tomb - Edgmond Church

There was another claimant besides Mrs Minor the newspaper recounting a story on the 25 June of a Mr Harper from London who like Mrs Minor had been deliberately cut out. Mr Harper claimed that the farm in Woodseaves was his as heir at law and had already informed the tenants. The story was that the Harper in question was so displeased with his son because he had joined the Methodists that he cut him off and left the estate to others listing five people to whom it should descend until all male heirs failed. The five lines of descent having now failed Mr Harper of London felt his line should be reinstated. The Advertiser saw in all this the vengeful hand of God the return of righteousness and a just reward for the possession of ill gotten gains!

Mrs Minor put her trust in the law she challenged the Harper Adams trustees in the Probate and Divorce Court in the case of Boughey and others v Minor. The trustees, Boughey in particular, not finding the will or Harper Adams personally attractive were keen to treat with Mrs Minor. They acknowledged that the property of the deceased came very largely from the family of the deceased's niece, that is the defendant Mrs Minor, who had been excluded from all benefits of the will. They had considered that the circumstances required them to look into the matter and to act fairly to the niece while observing the wishes of the deceased. They had therefore agreed for the niece to take that portion of the estate that descended from her mother. The Attorney general had agreed it was right and proper so that the portion the niece would receive would be between £15,000-£16,000 which would represent the amount of her late mother's property. This case and judgement would give the solemn approval to these arrangements. After giving up the amount she already received Mrs Minor would get between £11,000 and £12,000. Liddle said the testator was sound in mind when the will was signed nevertheless the Judge agreed the terms should be placed on file. After 52 years Mrs Minor had laid to rest an obsession.

At the sale Mrs Minor bought Edgmond House, to which she retired in 1896, and pasture land for £2,650 and died there aged 78 in 1915. John Minor had died in 1908; there were no children. Her property was inherited by Henry John Minor Kilvert Minor Adams who took her name as a condition of the will. In 1918 he sold the warehouse in Stafford Street formerly the wool warehouse of the Blakemores and the following year farms at Prees, Whixall and Cheswardine. In 1920 Town House in Newport High Street, now the Literary Institute was offered for sale and in 1926 Adams House itself plus 7, 8 and 11 High Street and 17 acres of pasture behind Adams House. In a long, roundabout way the Blakemores recovered the value of their property.

The obsession of the brothers in retaining what they had accumulated, in excluding others who might dilute this inheritance, their anxiety to achieve the social prestige and status they lacked in life, lead them to a wealthy dead end. There was literally no one left, leaving their money to a public institution would keep it intact would thwart those they disliked, so in one malevolent gesture Harper Adams created from his sinister attributes a philanthropic monument that none could deny. Who cares today that from the wrong reason came the right result, an institution that serves its students, the agricultural industry, the local community and is of national and international significance - Harper Adams University College.

Oh Danny Boy

"The Irishman is a carefree, cheerful, potato-eating child of nature"

Engels, Friedrich.,
"The Condition of the Working Class in England". 1845

In 1841 there were few Irish living in Newport even if you include one poor soul, Ann Ankers aged 55, in the workhouse. There was James Allen a brazier in Watkins Yard obviously working with John Watkins, a brazier, after whom the Yard was named. In the same Yard was John Morris aged 40 a hawker with an Irish wife but with all his children under the age of 10 born in Shropshire. Thomas Morris, aged 25, a stone mason, with his young wife and daughter from Shropshire, and a lodger John Freeman, another stone mason, was in St Marys Street as was Thomas Prentice a fellmonger aged 30 and Andrew Cureton, another hawker, with an Irish wife and son but with four other children under 14 all from Shropshire. Michael Duffy, a hawker and Joseph Caswell, a sawyer both had wives, and children under 14, born in the county. James Veitch and his Shropshire wife were landlords of the Crown Inn in the High Street one of the largest in the town.

These few Irish all had trades and skills and had long been domiciled in Shropshire. This small number is perhaps surprising given that Newport was on the main road to Ireland which was then part of the United Kingdom with Irish MP`s sitting in Westminster. Along the road went the administrators, the politicians and the military and the famous including Dean Swift, who on his journey from Dublin stayed at the Bear Inn and scratched his name on the bedroom wall.

The England of the 1840`s, was a time of riots and violence, strikes and demonstrations, political agitation with the Anti-Corn Laws, parliamentary reform and the Chartists, led by an Irishman, Feargus O`Connor, and was not an attractive decade even for impoverished Irishmen. There had been food riots on the Telford coalfields and local shortages were frequent not for nothing was the decade known as the "Hungry Forties". The population of Newport had declined by nearly three hundred between 1831 and 1841.

In other parts of the country the Irish had been coming for years sometimes to settle but often as itinerant workers on farms, canals and then railways. For generations their labour had fuelled the industrial revolution in Lancashire earning the lowest wages, doing the dirtiest work and living in the poorest housing, tolerated as long as they did the jobs no-one else could or would do. Their wages were essential to their families back in Ireland.

The harvest had brought the Irish - who all seemed to be called Patrick, Michael, James, John or Thomas - down the A41 and they were as much a part of the scene as the crops themselves. They slept on the farms doing their own washing and cooking at open fires. Wild looking and incomprehensible to the locals they stuck together carrying their possessions in blue and white handkerchiefs over their shoulders on the end of a stick, determined to earn as much as they could to send home, drinking on Saturday nights followed by Mass on the Sunday no matter how far the walk to church. They were young, strong and generally inoffensive. Newport had its own Catholic church, priest and school protected by local catholic landowners and while the Irish were few, seasonal and itinerant, they were not regarded as a threat.

In the 1840's they came as "navvies" on the railways providing at least a third of the workforce. Though living in separate camps provided by the contractors they were frequently attacked by the Scottish and English labourers and used as an attacking force by the less scrupulous contractors - even Brunel - against other railway companies. The violence and the fear experienced on the Scottish border and Somerset and at Wolverhampton was missing on Shropshire railways most of which had been completed by 1850. In Penrith, Carlisle, Kendal and Edinburgh, "randies" - drunken spells - and riots had become habitual requiring magistrates, police and troops. A long way from Shropshire, nevertheless the awesome legend of the navvies, and the Irish in particular, seen as barbarious, dirty, feckless and alien, spread fear amongst the middle classes and was used to frighten the children into behaving. The reputation of the Irish may have been sensationalised but it was not helped by the public execution of three Catholic Irish highwaymen in Shrewsbury in August 1836 with 10,000 spectators, some from Newport.

By 1851 the picture had radically changed with nearly 300 Irish in Newport out of a population of 2,906, about 10%. In 1841 there had been no Irish in the fourteen houses in Bellmans Yard but in 1851 with two houses unoccupied out of 129 residents 74 were Irish and 71 of these were crowded in three houses. Fifty six were under thirty. Only one had been born in Newport so the influx had been huge and recent. In the High Street, in three houses, there were 64 Irish, 53 under thirty with 7 children born in the town within the year, again a very dramatic and rapid influx. In two houses in Stafford Street were 29 Irish all under thirty including 7 children; in Marsh Lane in four households were 55 Irish, 15 under the age of ten five being born in Newport; in Cock Yard out of fourteen houses one was occupied by 17 Irish 10 of whom were lodgers and 2 babies. 118 gave their occupation as "agricultural labourer".

The 1851 census also reveals that in the Madeley Poor Law District - Madeley, Shifnal and Wellington - there was also a large Irish settlement, again, like Newport, in clusters as in Nailors Row and New Street in Wellington.

Bellmans Yard, a narrow lane giving access from the High Street to the Marsh, is now mostly demolished, but the cottages that remain indicate at the most two bedrooms, more likely a bedroom and a landing. They were occupied by John Grimes, John Walsh and William Walsh and their families but in fact they were packed with "lodgers", 52 in all. Where on earth did they eat and sleep or was this just a convenience of the census enumerator since the Irish had to be named, counted and given a residence to satisfy the law? The pattern is repeated in Marsh Lane, the High Street, Stafford Street and Cock Yard where out of 168 Irish occupants 116 were "lodgers", 69%. Here again we have the rapid, mass, evacuation of an impoverished, illiterate, catholic, homeless and unskilled people. These were a different breed to the Irish seen in Newport before 1850, these were Spalpeens, migratory labourers from the rural poor, a word that came to mean a rascal, a fellow who made trouble, someone viewed with suspicion and distrust.

The cause of this massive change in the pattern of migration was the Irish potato famine. Famine is a word associated with third world countries but was a feature of life in most of Europe up to 1800. Local shortages of food were worsened by the lack of transport from areas of plenty. There had been famine in Ireland in 1739-40, bread riots on the Coalbrookdale coalfield in 1756 and 1782 and in 1815 bakers and millers in Newport had been forced to issue a public notice to explain the price of flour and bread in order to prevent social unrest.

Bellmans Yard

In 1845 the potato disease spread from southern England to Ireland and by 1846 one in four acres were ruined. It was estimated that four million people in Ireland and two million in the United Kingdom lived off the potato. Also in 1845 the oats and corn harvests were also poor. In 1847 the harvests were better but by then the population was devastated by weakness and starvation and deaths continued. Immigration from Ireland reached its peak about 1857 and if we look at the 1861 census this is certainly true of Newport. Between two to three million settled in England, most were assimilated but many moved on in a second wave of emigration, to Canada and the United States, in the 1880's.

In 1861 there are 512 Irish in Newport out of a population of 3,051 that is 16.78%. Without this inflow of migrants Newport's population would have shrunk by about 400 which explains why there was plenty of unoccupied property for them to settle. In Bellmans Yard there were 113 Irish that is 81 giving Ireland as their origin and 32 born in Newport. 81 were under the age of 30 and 52 still gave their occupation as agricultural labourer. They occupied twenty houses out of twenty four. The 1851 census had only listed fourteen houses. In Marsh Lane there were 59 households of which thirty were Irish with 80 of Irish birth and 46 born in the town after arrival. A total of 128 Irish. One hundred were under thirty and 49 gave their occupation as agricultural labourer. In 1851 there had been only four Irish households in Marsh Lane with 55 Irish.

The number of Irish households in 1861 had increased to 9 in Stafford Street with 25 of Irish birth and 25 born since arrival, making 50 of whom 32 (64%) were under thirty. Fifteen worked on farms. Beaumaris Lane had a cluster of eight households with 44 Irish over 70% under thirty, 16 being agricultural labourers. Cock Yard was now crowded with nine out of eighteen homes occupied by 44 Irish nearly 100% being under 30 and 13 in farming. Watery Lane had five houses with 21 Irish, 16 under thirty and 6 working on the land. So here we have an increased Irish population clustered in the poorest areas of the town, very young with a larger percentage of first generation born in Newport.

Prosperity had returned to England and to Newport by 1860 illustrated by the increased investment in the regeneration of the town, with new streets, Stafford Street, New Street, Avenue Road; cattle removed from the streets into purpose built livestock markets and a new market hall; the infected churchyard closed and the dead removed to a new cemetery; a new workhouse; and the new (1848) railway. Alongside this confidence was the presence of these large numbers of Irish undermining the image the town had worked hard to improve.

By 1855 the White Lion a beer house had become an enclave of the Irish in Bellmans Yard and was run by Morris O`Shaughnessy himself. On Saturday 9 October that year there came a fracas which led to the withdrawal of its license when the police found over forty men and women drunk, obstructing the pavement and so riotous they were heard by Mr Liddle the solicitor of Town House across the road. Peter Kelly, the Irish waiter, swore he saw no drunks or any quarrelling and fighting but his myopia was to no avail as the magistrates proved the case but let them off with a caution as it was a first offence.

In August 1857 at a Wakes Week dance down the road at the Fox and Duck, Pave Lane, a group of Irish took on the locals threatening the landlord, Mr Mancell, and his daughter with sickles, smashing windows and beds and ending with deep wounds and beaten bodies, the Irish apparently coming off worst.

In August 1858 the Irish burst out from the heat and stench of their crowded yards, many bringing their chairs to sit in the cool of the High Street. On the seventh of August, a Sunday evening just as the church congregations were assembling at their relevant churches one of these "disgraceful and disgusting" street rows began when about fifty Irish men, women and children congregated in one spot to pick quarrels with each other with one "dastardly and cowardly" chap assaulting another. Apparently this sort of behaviour had become frequent on Sunday evenings around the Cock Yard, Bellmans Yard and at the end of Stafford Street where, as we have seen, there were great numbers of Irish, who stopped up the pavements, prevented pedestrians walking and frightened the neighbours to death. Where were the police it was asked, to stop such demoralising and degrading scenes? A week later Edward McCloughlin an Irish labourer was charged with stealing 1/6 (7.5p) from Fieldings the grocers in the High Street who withdrew the charge. Was this because of the unrest it might have stirred up? While in the lock-up in the Town Hall, Edward amused himself by pulling all the whitewash and the plaster off the wall.

On the 28 August the Newport Advertiser reported another row on the Sunday when up to 200 Irish congregated at different parts of the town and later in the evening merged into one large, dangerous, crowd armed with pokers, stones and various missiles preventing the peaceful inhabitants using the street. The stern, pious, nonconformist editor again deplored such disreputable behaviour and called on the police and the parish constables to act.

One Irishman, Edward Kelly, responded by getting drunk and disorderly in Bellmans Yard for which he was fined 5/- (25p) and 6/- costs (30p). He paid immediately!

There were a goodly number of other Novaportans drunk and disorderly but being new and distinctive the Irish caught the attention as the Advertiser reported in January 1882 after the usual New Years Eve disturbances. Again the centre was Bellmans Yard and the White Lion on a Tuesday afternoon in January after the Petty Sessions, when the drunks from New Years Eve had been sentenced and sent to prison in default of paying fines. Two, Judge and Simpson, were drunk in court and had to be put in the lock-up. Around 4 o`clock it was decided to take the prisoners to the railway station en route to Shrewsbury prison a run that had to be made down Stafford Street, High St - past Bellmans Yard - Station Road to the railway; it had all the features of a Western film. The police sergeant, three constables and the Assistant Chief Constable set out in an orderly manner until they reached the Yard where the prisoner`s friends stood with foaming jugs of beer. The sergeant smashed the jug with his stick and an "unseemly quarrel" resulted, the police using batons the Irish stones and fists and the station was not reached without an ugly battle which ended when the station gates were locked. By this time, it is said, the prisoners were quite merry. Patrick Judge was a 23 year old farm labourer from Marsh Road. John Dever, a 19 year old Irish labourer and neighbour in Marsh Road, was also committed.

The petty session records are full of Irish men, women and children up for drunkenness, disorder, assault, obstruction and petty larceny.

From 1870 agriculture declined with competition from overseas particularly the USA and Canada. The main occupation of the early Irish immigrants was in farming so they were bound to feel the effect but the generation of Newport-born Irish were already moving into other trades and being young, they were in their mid-twenties by 1881, they were migrating like their parents, but this time out of Newport. On 16 April 1887 11 Irish, men and women, left Newport station to emigrate to the USA the agent being Peter Kelly. In 1888 Canon Rogerson, the Roman Catholic minister, with the Rector of Newport, raised funds to send two families to the USA or Canada sailing on the 'Sardinian' of the Allan Line from Liverpool on 12 April.

Tom Fahey (Foy) was born in the yard of the Honeysuckle Inn on 3 April 1866 the son of Thomas McCormick Fahey and Bridget who had come to Newport from Galway, Ireland in 1850. In 1881 they are at Marsh Lane (Audley Road) when Thomas was 15 and in 1891 the old couple are still there running a lodging house. Thomas attended the Roman Catholic school leaving at the age of 13 to work as an errand boy with Foxall and Williams, grocers, delivering with a horse and cart. At the age of 18 he went to Manchester emigrating from there aged 21 in 1887. He returned to Newport between 1895 and 1911 and married Mrs Mary Ann Frewer whom he had known as a child in Newport, being the daughter of James and Bridget Duffy Welsh who had also come from Ireland. Tom Foy died at Munn Road, Cleveland, Ohio on 29 April 1966 being exactly 100 years old.

Martin Moran was born in Ireland in 1840 and wandered around with his wife and family in Scotland in 1866, Newcastle under Lyme in 1869 and Newport in the 1870's. In 1889 he decided to go again this time to America where he would settle and send for his wife and four children in Bellmans Yard. He sailed from Liverpool to Philadelphia in July 1889 and then on to Chicago. Whether he intended to keep his promise to his family we shall never know as in December 1890 aged 50 he contrived to get struck by an engine on a level crossing and died later in the Mercy Hospital, Chicago.

The decline in the number of Irish was matched by the decline in the population of Newport. It was the arrival of the Irish that had prevented an even bigger drop in numbers, a drop that continued until 1914 and after. In 1881 Newport had dropped to 3044 and the Irish from 17% to 13%; in 1891 the figures were 2675 and the Irish 8%.

Many of the Newport Irish claimed kinship, coming from the west coast of Mayo, Clare, Galway and Westmeath, from towns like Galway, Castlebar, Roscommon and Westport. Early arrivals were Kelly, Grimes, Walsh, in its several varieties; later was Laby (1851-71), Nealon/Neales/Naylis (1871-91), Burk(e) (1851-71), Davy/Dover/Dever (1871-91), Kane/Cain/Keane (1851 until today), Boggin (1851/71) and Gerraughty, Shaughnessy, Kirkpatrick and Kilcoyne from 1871 until now (2010). By 1891 the majority had been born in Newport.

Michael Kane and his Irish wife Anne were living in Cock Yard in 1861 with their son Henry aged 3. They are still there in 1881 when Henry was working as a miller. In 1891 he was married to Margaret and living in Bellmans Yard and in 1901 he had moved to Beaumaris Road, his youngest child, of five, being Charles. In 1921 at Charles' wedding Henry is described as an engine driver at the Creamery in Forton Road. Bill Kane (2010) the son of Charles can remember visiting his grandmother Margaret after Mass, in her black bonnet in her little cottage in Bellmans Yard.

Another Kane (Keane), Roger, came over from Mayo in the 1850s and lived with his wife Bridget and son Richard in a cottage in the Blue Ball Yard in St Marys Street. By 1901 Richard with his Irish wife Mary Quinn was in the Marsh Road with their son Roger named after his Irish grandfather. Roger was Company Sergeant Major in the East Lancashire Regiment in the First World War, was a stalwart of the British Legion and the Home Guard and greeted Field Marshall Montgomery when he stopped in Newport in June 1949.

> "The cottages are old, dirty, and of the smallest sort. The streets uneven, fallen into ruts and in part without drains or pavements; masses of refuse, offal and sickening filth lie among standing pools in all directions....ruinous cottages, broken windows mended with oilskin, sprung doors and rotten doorposts...measureless filth and stench."

Engels, ibid describing the Irish in Manchester 1845.

From 1851 the Irish crowded into property that was already old and empty; in Water Lane and Marsh Lane, cottages and lodging houses backed onto the Marsh Brook, an open sewer, water coming from hydrants (standpipes) in the High Street. They found the property empty and dilapidated and left it like that, a report of 1907 indicating that no working class house had been built for years and the private owners, usually local business men, had no money to maintain them. Houses were void where the Irish had previously clustered. The birth rate was down, population down by 10%, again, wages low, rents declining. It is surprising, not that the Irish left, but that so many families stayed to be assimilated.

John Barrett, who had lived in Bellmans Yard since a boy, was still there in 1907 but most houses around him were void and the rest in poor condition with floors and roofs falling in. A few years later the magistrates ordered No. 6 Bellmans Yard to be vacated. It had one bedroom 15 feet by 12 feet divided by a partition with three beds in which there were 2 adults and eight children aged 2 years to 20. It was one of a group of houses unfit for habitation. Conditions had been worse in 1851. His wife, Bridget Barrett was a Walsh, (some say "Welch") having come with her parents as a nine months old baby in 1847 and had lived in Bellmans Yard ever since. In 1861 Bridget Walsh aged 18 from Ireland is living in Bellmans Yard with her parents Henry and Mary Walsh. She married John Barrett in 1871 and we find both, aged 24, and a one month old son John, lodging with her parents, Mary and Henry then aged 69. Mrs Barrett kept a lodging house in the Yard for 45 years and in 1901 she and her husband and two sons James and John are living in the same house with five lodgers. When James was born in 1873 Bridget signed the birth certificate with a X. John Barrett like so many others was a farm labourer and was later killed by a horse. Bridget died in April 1923 in Newport workhouse aged 77 very Irish and a fervent Catholic.

In sharp contrast is the story of Thomas Barrett, labourer, who in May 1856 married Mary Grimes aged 18 from Bellmans Yard, at SS Peter and Paul in Salters Lane, Newport. Both came from Ireland. In 1871 they had five children including one girl Mary Ann Barrett born in February 1863. By 1881 only Mary (Grimes) and her daughter Mary Ann and youngest son Patrick are at home and it must have at this time that like many others they decided to emigrate for by 1883 Mary Ann Barrett is in the United States. Soon after, she was joined by her mother. In Newport Mary Ann had met John McDonnell (McDonald?) who had been born in Scotland of Irish parents. In 1871 we find a Mary McDonnell aged 30 in Water Lane with an 11 year old son born in Scotland. Mary Ann and John were reunited in New York and married. Mary Ann died in 1957 aged 94 her progeny including lawyers, diplomats, government officials, educators and business executives a long way from Bellmans Yard and very different to Bridget's end in the workhouse.

The children reflect the true condition of these families. There was a charity school in 1842 probably in Salters Hall but it was the Rev. John Rogerson who came to Newport in 1872 from Birkenhead who built the Catholic school in 1879. For many years he struggled to finance the school and deal with the poverty and the ignorance, it revealed. Disease, absenteeism, sheer filth had to be overcome to convince parents of the value of education for which until 1891 they were expected to pay. Children were starving and hard winters and unemployment and the competition of the public house made things even worse in the 1890's.

The Irish were classed as "the very poor" and 87% of the children at the school were in that bracket. The reality was no boots and overcoats in which to come to school; the reality was simple things like books were always dirty because hands were never clean; children were verminous, with constant epidemics of ringworm, impetigo, measles, whooping cough, scabies, mumps, scarlet fever, chicken pox and colds which meant isolation at home as the only answer, however, absence meant children were always in the lower grades leaving school at 12 and 13 without knowing the alphabet. At one time only one child in the whole school was not suffering severe tooth decay.

Newport Catholic School 1898

Infant mortality rates, that is, under the age of one year, were high nationally, and in Newport, where they were 25% in 1851 and 34% in 1861. Many Irish children died in their first year between 1855 and 1859 casually referred to in the records as "Irish child", not until February 1859 is one named as 'Bridget Dougherty, Irish' aged 10 days.

Parents went to prison, if they were not already in prison, for keeping children at home to work or for neglect. Numbers were around 50 and many of these would not be Catholic. As the Irish families declined before 1914 so did numbers. The summers of 1912 and 1913 were extremely hot and underfed children showed alarming signs of fatigue, so it is no wonder there did not appear to be many naturally bright children. Gifts of clothing, simple treats, gardening and sewing brightened lives but real fitness and enjoyment had to wait until the 1930`s.

The Kellys were here in 1841 and still are (2010). They do not quite fit the pattern as John Kelly was here in 1841 and as he had a son aged 6 born in Wolverhampton, John must have been here as early as 1835. He was a hawker in haberdashery and they remained shopkeepers. John was born in Ireland in 1811 long before the famine and married Bridget in Ireland. Between 1833 and 1840 they lived in Wolverhampton though they knew Newport, being godparents to the child of a Mr and Mrs Murray at the Catholic Church in Newport in 1833. Their third son, Peter, was born in Newport in 1840 as were their subsequent children.

Bridget died in 1860 and John in 1873. The eldest son also John became a marine store dealer in Whitchurch.

Their daughter Mary married Michael Rafferty a general dealer living in Stafford Street. She is still there as a china shop keeper in 1901. Her daughter Kate Rafferty was a governess in Morocco but came home in 1914 to keep house for her Uncle Billy at 50 High Street.

Peter, the third child of John Kelly, went to America about 1860 and returned to England to marry Hannah Pritchard of Eyton-on-the-Weald Moors. Hannah died aged 73 in 1922 at Burleigh House, St Marys Street. Their son Frank Siberia Kelly was born on the Cunard liner "Siberia", on its journey back to England on 3 January 1870. The name has been used in the family as a second Christian name ever since. There was already a little colony of former Novaportans around Chicago including the Edwards brothers from the "Crow", next to the Grammar School. The younger Kelly brother, Thomas, at the age of 18 went to Cleveland where his daughter married a Mr Anderson in Tacoma, Washington.

Burleigh House
Courtesy the Kelly family

Peter went on to be a boot and shoe dealer, draper and clothier and to accumulate property in the town. He was the agent to the "American Line" dealing with emigration. In April 1889 he bought 137 High St, formerly the "Three Fishes" beer house, and five cottages in Water Lane. Number 137 was rebuilt by Whittinghams as two shops with a house over and its distinctive design is still visible. He also bought the curriers shop of Sarjeants next door which was burnt down in 1903 and rebuilt as offices for the Urban District Council and is now (2010) the Youth Café. In 1900 just before he died he rebuilt 2 St Marys Street the builder being Muirhead who used red bricks left over from his contract with Harper Adams College. They can still be seen in the alley leading to the market. He also acquired 69 High Street, later Greenwoods and 99A High Street and nine cottages in Watkins Yard.

Kelly's Shop, 2 St. Mary's Street

31

William Kelly the seventh child of John lived with his father at the Marine Stores in Stafford Street and carried on after the death of his father mainly at 50 High Street, known as the "Unicorn Buildings" after the former public house, where he died in 1925 when he was described as a clothier and shipping agent, "an able business man". He was buried a Roman Catholic. Billy was a member of the Albrighton Hunt and his horse "Clinker" was buried in the garden.

Frank Siberia Kelly the son of Peter, grandson of John, died in 1931. He had two large families and an even larger portfolio of property including nos 2 and 4 and Burleigh House in St Marys Street, houses in Water Lane, Avenue Road South, Vineyard Road, Lilleshall, Chetwynd End and Beaumaris Road and fields in Victoria Park, the Sandhole, Almshouse Field and also the Tanyard. Though they took little part in public life they were well known and exceedingly popular, in three generations they had become part of the fabric of Newport.

Michael James Kilcoyne was born in Ireland about 1850 and his parents, Michael and Catherine, with their three eldest children immigrated to Newport shortly after his birth where they had three more children. In the 1861 census Michael has died and Catherine, aged 45 is listed as the 'Head' of the household, an agricultural labourer with six children; Michael was eleven years old; soon after the family relocated to the Scranton area of Pennsylvania. Catherine Toole Kilcoyne sailed with her daughter Bridget, a deaf mute, Anthony, who became a prominent priest and Mary, on the first of May 1865 on the Caledonia, probably from Glasgow. By 1870 the family, the three older boys having gone out earlier, are all together in Scranton. In 1875 Michael married Margaret Lavelle who had been born in Scranton in 1856 the daughter of Michael and Mary Lavelle. Lavelles were also in Newport at this time. When Margaret died in 1898 aged 42 she left ten children whom Michael abandoned and remained estranged from them until his death in 1915 in Shamokin, Pennsylvania.

Fortunately there were also heroes. Patrick Kilcoyne an Irish farm labourer aged 27 lodged with Mary Grimes in Bellmans Yard in 1881. Next door was Honor Geraughty, aged 20, daughter of John Geraughty and Bridget, also farm workers from Ireland. By 1891 Patrick and Honor were married with six sons and a daughter Mary. Father-in-law John and his three strapping sons also lodged with them in Bellmans Yard. Patrick had come to England at the age of 18 as a harvester, returning at the seasons end. By 1874 he had settled permanently working on the farm of Mrs Winnall at Brockton Leasowes then as a nurseryman on the Lilleshall Estate and, after that was sold, with Mr George Hull at Muxton Grange Farm now the Golf Club. The third son was Patrick also, born in 1887. Being good Catholics the Kilcoyne children attended the Catholic school and were noted for their regular attendance despite the reputation, as recorded in the school log book, of "the usual set from Bellmans Yard". In November 1905 the only daughter, Mary, was absent from school nursing her mother who died the following month probably in child birth.

The records show that Patrick Kilcoyne was one of the first to enlist in Shrewsbury on the 29 August 1914 and became Lance Corporal 11356 in "D" Company of the 5th Battalion of the Kings Shropshire Light Infantry and that he died of wounds in England in June 1916 aged 29 and is buried in Newport cemetery. His death, being one of the first casualties in Newport, brought an overwhelming effusion of grief an outpouring that was not repeated as the war continued and death became commonplace. Patrick had taken part in the battle of Loos but it was during the attack on the Hohenzollern redoubt in September 1915 that he was badly wounded. He was brought back to a hospital in Manchester where he died. The death cast an extraordinary gloom over the town and district where he was well known and highly respected and was a devout Catholic. Loveable and well living he was a good athlete and footballer playing for Edgmond and the Early Closers, and his life promised much. He left school to become an errand boy but then worked at the Advertiser office but at the time of his enlistment he was working for the Audley Engineering Company.

On that Wednesday night a large assembly of family and townspeople gathered at the railway station and on the bridge to await the 8.20 pm train from Stafford bringing the body, but it was not until several trains later, at 11 pm that it arrived on the mail train from Stafford. Some two to three hundred people were waiting when the train steamed in and the scene when the body was brought out of the train and placed on a wheeled bier for the drive through the town was very emotional. As the cortege with its military escort proceeded the streets were lined with crowds, the men with heads uncovered, the women tearful. The body was met at the entrance to the Roman Catholic Church by the Rev. Giles and the Rev Dr. Hazelhurst who said the Dei Profundis and where it remained all night.

33

Funeral of Patrick Kilcoyne - 24th June 1916

The funeral took place on the Thursday afternoon after the church service the procession being led by the Grammar School Cadets led by the Headmaster (Captain) J.W.Shuker and one of the masters, Lt J.E.Gill. Other military followed. The coffin was covered with the Union Jack and carried on a bier escorted by the Shropshire Light Infantry. The chief mourners were Patrick Kilcoyne (senior), three brothers and two sisters with representatives from Audley Engineering, including Mr R Leach, the managing director, the football clubs and five or six hundred townsfolk. The route was from Salters Lane, along the High Street to Audley Avenue, with shop blinds drawn, flags at half mast, the pavements lined by friends and neighbours and the schoolchildren drawn up in front of the Avenue Road school. The ceremony ended with two buglers sounding the Last Post.

Two months earlier a rebellion, the Easter Rising, had taken place in Dublin with serious street fighting, loss of life and the summary execution of the leaders after the expected German aid did not arrive.

On the afternoon of 8 December 1939 the children of SS Peter and Paul School met to dance and sing songs to celebrate the visit of Pat Melia an "old boy" of the school who had been torpedoed on HMS Gypsy and was home on leave. Ordinary Seaman George Edward Patrick Melia, the 19 year old son of Mr and Mrs Edward Melia of Vauxhall Terrace and formerly Church Aston, was the youngest member of the crew of the destroyer HMS Gypsy which had been sunk by a magnetic mine on 22 November but fortunately was not seriously injured. He was Newport's first victim of the Second World War.

The Melia's had come from Ireland to Newport in at least the 1870's and Edward Melia had served for 22 years, until 1929, as an Able Seaman in the navy and had been in the crew of HMS Cressy which had been torpedoed and sunk during the Great War. Patrick had followed his dad at the age of fifteen.

He gave a graphic account of lying in his hammock about 9.30 in the evening when a terrific explosion shook the ship from stem to stern and he was hurled onto the deck with some force. Soon the dynamos exploded and the ship heeled over. Dazed and bleeding Pat rushed on deck and plunged into the icy water the ship then being on its beam ends in the thick, oily, sea. After twenty minutes swimming he reached land with about thirty other members of the crew. Helpers walked him into town and the naval hospital, covered in oil and dressed only in trousers and a thin vest, cold and miserable. Two days later he was on 14 days leave in Newport. His parents heard the news on the radio but then messages came by telegram and it was a long, anxious, wait until the Friday morning before they knew their son was safe.

Ninety years after arriving hungry and destitute the Irish were at home and Newport was grateful.

"The Sudden and Furyous Fire."

In May 1665 Thomas Munk, Parish Clerk of Newport, was upset, and his entry in the Parish Register was terse and to the point. He was no Samual Pepys and the fire he was lamenting was no Fire of London of the following year, yet what happened on the 19 May 1665 was as disastrous for Newport and proved the old adage that fire is a wonderful servant but a nasty master. Of course the technology to tackle fires did not exist but there was also lack of organisation and indifference until the next outbreak when there was again a bustle of activity and suggestions until the alarm wore off. So it was that fire remained a shocking event in Newport until the Second World War when the town was forced into reality.

Site of the Red Lion

"Memorandum that on the ffridaye in the afternoone beeinge the 19 daye of May Anno 1665 a sudden furyous fire arose which began in the house of Richard Shelton a smith living at the Antelope (Chitlop) whiche by Saturdaye noone following were burned out of habitation about 162 familyes besides the better of 10 more of houses puld to pieces and much prevented. Thos. Munk (Parish Clerk and Registrar)."

The Minister of the church the Rev. Thomas Millington, drew a moral from the fire but also overestimated the loss at £30,000 as a good fundraising vicar should: "Newport sin no more lest a worse punishment b'fall thee. The losse to Newport was 30000 poundes."

In a hand written note by the Earl of Shrewsbury in a presentation book, are more precise details and costings: "On the 19th of May in 17 Car.II. a dreadful fire broke out in this town about four in the afternoon which in the space of a few hours consumed more than 156 habitations most of the best houses in the body of the town with all the malthouses, barns and stables belonging to them together with the old Market House and part of the new and almost all the goods and furniture, money, plate, liquors and provision to the amount of £23,948 viz. £12,948 for the building £11,000 for the goods etc: a brief was issued for the relief of the sufferers on the 15th October 18 Car.II."

The brief issued by the King asked everyone in the country to be generous and indicates how frequent such tragedies were, and hoped Christian compassion would not be lessened "because deplorable objects of this nature are often exhibited to them." Oliver Cromwell had issued similar briefs for fires in Glasgow in 1652 and Malborough the following year. Locally there had been a fire in Shifnal in 1591 when 32 houses were destroyed and the large church severely damaged, a fire which radically altered the pattern of the town; there was a fire in Wrexham in 1643 which destroyed a quarter of the town; there was a fire in Wem in 1677 when most of the earlier buildings were destroyed and in Oswestry in 1742 which left few buildings before the eighteenth century.

The King's brief gave the inhabitants of Newport the right to solicit and receive donations from all over the Kingdom, inhabitants, it said, who were "at mid-day full and flourishing" and were "before mid-night deprived of all, made empty and nothing, compelled to lodge in open air and to seek hospitality, food and necessaries at the hands of others." Certificates supporting their plea were issued at the Shrewsbury Quarter Sessions by the Justices of the Peace Lord Newport, Sir Thomas

Wolryche, Sir Richard Otley, Francis Thornes, Robert Owen, Charles Baldwyn, Adam Otley and Thomas Baudewin. It then describes who was to receive the money in London and the local committee empowered to assess claims and distribute the money according to their "several poverties, and to the proportion of each of their several losses…"

We do know individual losses, the inventory of Walter Astley in 1666 listing goods which were "the residue and remainder….which are now left undestroyed by ye late ruins of fire which happened in Newport….including part of his clothes and wearing apparel and ye rest burnt." While we may not know exactly what was collected we do have a record of some contributions; from Staunton in Oxfordshire in 1668, 4/1d. (20p); collected in Sparsholt in Berkshire 6/3. (31p); collected in Ludlow £1.03.04. (1.17p); at St Nicholas, Durham, £1.06.08. (1.36p) and at Rotherfield, Sussex, 13/8. (88p). In the accounts of the churchwardens of St Mary, Leicester in 1667 we find "for Newporte in Shrop Shire the 24th of March £1.6s.4d."

Traditionally the site of the fire, the Antelope, later called the Red Lion, has been held to be the present site of Barclay's Bank in the High Street and despite the efforts of later amateur historians there seems little reason to dispute this. With so much later rebuilding or the addition of new facades and street extensions and infilling, it is difficult to trace the exact area of the fire or to believe it was as extensive as the 1665 petitioners made out. Was it around the church of St Nicholas or the older part of Upper Bar? 156 houses destroyed in Upper Bar seems rather a lot for such a small area? Older properties survived such as the Guildhall and Smallwood Lodge in the south of the town while the Butter Market in the centre was burnt down and rebuilt and the new brick Market Hall on the town square (1662) survived as did the new brick building of the Grammar School, built 1656. The church appears untouched.

Whatever the extent, as in London after 1666, the town was rebuilt on the same pattern of the original Norman town the Butter Market (Butter Cross) for example was replaced by Thomas Talbot as early as November 1665. But myths will continue, the finding of charred timbers in fields beyond Beaumaris Road leading to the idea that the town was originally there, while others have suggested the reason for the wide High Street is that the fire destroyed the shops and houses that previously ran down the middle!

Fire needed water, it needed equipment and it needed organisation and these were lacking until modern times. In 1665 there was a good supply of water from the wells in Church Aston but this was little more than a trickle into cisterns placed around the town. They were controlled by the Burgesses an ancient body, inefficient, absentee unable for years to carry out their duties. There was also the Parish based on the area around the church run by meetings in the vestry at which everyone could be present though in fact it was usually a small number of influential townspeople presided over by the clergyman. They could raise money but their duties covered everything, the poor, highways, law and order, sanitation and these increased over the years. Carrying out such duties was unpopular, contentious and often dangerous and raising money through the rates was often avoided if money could be raised by subscription. So for generations subscriptions rather than compulsory rates were used to pay for repairing the roads, paying the church organist, buying a new church clock, building schools and repairing or buying a fire engine.

As time went on life became even more complicated as regards fire prevention. Whose job was it, the Burgesses, the parish, the Lord of the Manor, the Marsh Trust after 1764 or the Guardians after 1834? Before we become too critical of a small country town we have to remember that there was no public fire brigade in London until 1865. Preventing fire was fairly hopeless and though authorities could regulate rebuilding insisting on brick dividing walls and tiled roofs they could not alter the pattern of building so properties remained crowded and hazardous and even brick built premises were not fireproof. You could be vigilant with night watchmen and Watch and Ward systems but there were no water pumps and equipment consisted of buckets, ladders and grab-hooks usually kept in the church. From 1665 there was an increased use of gunpowder to create fire breaks. Given this it is remarkable how quickly people recovered, London was rebuilt within one year and its churches by the 1680`s.

In 1699 the Parish was the authority for tackling fires and in that year fire hooks were placed in the rebuilt Market Hall. The Churchwardens accounts for 1702 show there was a fire in the church steeple after which 2/- was paid for ale and 3d to a man named Perridge who put the fire out. In 1743 a new fire engine was bought in London for £50 and kept in the church. Another new engine was purchased in 1766 for £20 and the old tub engine of 1743, from Mr Browne of Newport, a plumber. In 1774 the parish purchased 16 leather buckets for fire.

However on the 8 October 1791 at noon a serious fire occurred in the vicinity of the tan yard in Water Lane. It spread rapidly along Marsh Lane (Audley Road) and up Bakehouse Lane (Stafford Street) a road so called because all the bake ovens were collected there ironically to lessen the danger of fire in the town. It was thought possible it would have reached the High Street had not two houses been pulled down to check its progress. The fire consumed the greater part of the tannery owned by the Alcock family with 55 tons of bark, 20 barns and stables, 18 dwelling houses amongst which was a beautiful mansion house belonging to a Captain Wigby, situated on Mount Pleasant. It also burnt down a drinking house and pleasure garden at the rear of the Horse and Jockey in St Marys Street and the Queens Head a public house which stood on the field opposite to the present New Inn. Deeds show barns being burned and replaced by cottages and Market Company deeds show them sixty years later buying property at the bottom of Bakehouse Lane which in 1792 was sold by William Rider to Thomas Dickenson consisting of 200 square yards formerly one house then four, lately burned down or consumed in part by fire. Rider was to forgo any money from the committee set up to distribute relief to the victims of the fire. The total damage was estimated at £1,850 and to meet this loss a subscription was heavily taken up throughout the neighbourhood and the amount was soon raised.

One man prominent in the 1791 fire was Silas Griffin a carpenter who came to work on the building of Longford Hall, settled in Newport and had his own business as well as the carpentry work on the Chetwynd Estate. It was he who used gunpowder to blow up the houses to stop the fire spreading. Silas was the grandfather of T.W.Picken who one hundred years later described the part his grandfather played. He says his grandfather, a master tradesman, was instrumental, with others, in checking the fire which began through sparks from a chimney setting light to straw thatch on a cottage. It was stopped when two houses were demolished by gunpowder and then pulled to pieces. His grandfather's knowledge meant he took a prominent part in the destruction of the houses. He was described by his daughter, Picken's mother, as a tall, powerful, and very courageous person who once rescued a man from drowning in Moss Pool. Coming home from the fire he was so overcome with excitement and fatigue, so begrimed with smoke, soot and dirt, that his own children did not know him.

In 1835 another engine was bought by public subscription but it proved too big for the church so wider doors had to be put in the vestry. By now the churchyard was sinking and it was difficult to get the engine out particularly at night, so central premises were rented behind the Butter Cross at £6 pa, the parish paying. As usual some objected that this was an illegal payment but it hardly mattered as the parish frequently did not pay the rent and in 1867 the owner of the engine house threatened to sell the engine to cover the back rent. In 1935 this old engine was still in the Urban District Council yard. Another subscription was raised in 1856 to renew hoses which were leather and over 20 years old, the fire insurance companies being the main subscribers.

Millwood Mere

By now a revolution had taken place in the water supply which previously ran from wells in Church Aston, through two inch lead pipes to cisterns. About 1840 the Burgesses used money from the sale of land to the canal company to improve the mains, put in street hydrants and supply private taps into property that could afford it, charging rents which went back into improving the system. The hydrants could have enough pressure to throw a jet of water but they did not cover the whole town. At the same time a reservoir was constructed, now Millwood Mere, which at a time of fire, could be connected to the mains.

These were constructed by the Massey family who were later to become superintendents of a proper fire brigade. The engine was still controlled by the parish and was tested occasionally at the election of churchwardens. However in 1867 it was transferred from the churchwardens to the overseers and paid for out of the parish rates. There was still no formal brigade anyone jumping on to the engine including the local roughs who saw it as an opportunity for a bit of excitement. The next year a brigade of 10-15 men was drilled and trained from the ranks of the Volunteer Rifle Corps which had been formed in 1862 at the time of the American Civil War. In 1870 the small fire engine was still locked up under the vestry in the church.

We have to remember that the local "roughs" or sightseers often became essential volunteers since a manual engine could require 16 men either side, that is, 32 men to work the handles of the pump.

Fires continued, one occurring at the windmill at the side of the canal and the Strine at Broomfield in December 1855 at three in the morning. The Windmill contained the turning and bending workshops of Mr Lewis Allkins with warehouses and living accommodation adjoining. The timber contents and timber frame were soon alight and after three hours three warehouses and two shops were completely gutted. The fire engine under Mr. T. Morris jnr, was soon on the scene followed by "many of the inhabitants who left their beds and went to the scene of the conflagration which lighted up the heavens around". The great damage and loss was alleviated by the custom of raising subscriptions this one headed by J.F.F.Boughey. Even so, Mr Allkin had to sell up.

There was a fire at Wilbrighton farm on the Aqualate estate in September 1858 when the tenant, Mr Allan, had twenty harvest stacks burnt down. Engines came from Newport, Aqualate and Lilleshall and a huge crowd gathered, estimated at 1,800 some to help most to watch. The blaze was clearly visible from Aqualate Hall and Sir T.F.F.Boughey came over the fields to take charge. In fact the flames could be seen at Stafford and Shrewsbury. In June 1862 there was another fire in a stackyard in Brineton through the natural heating of the hay, the farmer, Mr Lee, having to ride into Newport to fetch the brigade. Four horses were harnessed and took the engine and the brigade to Brineton "in no time". It was said that the engine was in excellent order, did good service and prevented damage to other stores and buildings.

On Saturday 6 August 1870 came a fire which not only threatened the safety of Newport but considerably jolted its pride for it occurred in the Market Hall or Town Hall a new, handsome building, the chief ornament of the town. Many feared that the fire would equal that of 1665. The building had been completed in 1860 and was one of the many civic improvements carried out in the prosperous years of the 1850`s and 60`s. Behind it was the livestock market which got the cattle off the streets and has only recently been demolished (2005/6). The building housed the indoor markets, still there, and at the front a two storey block with shops, a butchers market, other rooms and an entrance from which led a broad stone staircase up to the assembly room. This fine chamber extended nearly across the length of the building lit by five large windows by day and at night by two gasoliers bringing a soft, white, light to the dancers on the admirable floor. It was this assembly room that was wrecked.

The fire was spotted at 10 o'clock at night when people were still shopping and began in the cupola which was then over the south-east corner of the building. The glare quickly illuminated the railway station at the southern end and Chetwynd woods at the northern. It threatened the huge stores of wines and spirits at the Vine Vaults thirty feet away, and the old, timbered houses in St Mary`s Street. It was also suspected that various innkeepers had large stores of spirits in the cellars of the Town Hall. Soon the fire had spread from the cupola and enveloped the front clock and the roof and large quantities of tiles and burning timber crashed down but luckily were held by the ballroom floor so that the ground floor never caught light.

For the first hour the large crowd – people still shopped and passed by in their carts - had no reason to doubt that the whole town would be ignited as the Newport engine was powerless and in fact failed ignominiously, while the engine brought in from Aqualate Park, then the engine of the Duke of Sutherland and that of the Lilleshall Company from Donnington Wood, stood helpless for lack of water. This scarcity was partly because of the drought that year but mainly because the public supply was inadequate for normal purpose never mind an emergency. For a long time it was even suggested that the paving stones be ripped up and used to attack the fire!

The big crowd looked on helplessly few knew what to do and there was no organisation, just a few brave deeds. Two people were slightly injured. Fortunately the assembly floor held, the outside walls stood and the building was saved. This was due to the efforts of Mr G Holland the local agent of the Sun Fire Office which covered the building for £3,000 and who sent for the fire brigades. Then the questions started, what had caused the fire why was the response and the water supply so inefficient? The engine and the brigade were inadequate but this was a problem for the whole neighbourhood not just the town as five out of six fires occurred in the surrounding countryside. Many felt that fire should be tackled on a county basis out of a county rate something that had to wait 70 years. As for water the supply had to be improved but this required not just new technology but new forms of government and this was resisted by the townspeople for thirty years.

Market Hall showing cupola where the fire began

Who caused the fire? It appears several boys were in the habit on a Saturday night of entering the cupola at the top of the Market Hall which was left unlocked and used gunpowder and matches to scare the pigeons. Unfortunately this ignited the sawdust put down to absorb the damp. As no malice was intended it was treated as an accident. The legends persist, one lady in 1988 maintaining that her grandfather who was 9 years old at the time of the fire, remembered it burning and saw people jumping from the roof!

Of course there was a post mortem at the end of August 1870 to discuss the fire engine which was still the 1867 one run by the parish overseers and paid for out of the parish rate. It was estimated that £80 would be needed for repairs as there had been little maintenance or supervision. A committee was appointed to discuss the deficiencies of the engine and to promote subscriptions as some were still against the cost being put on the rates. They thought of purchasing new hose and even a second engine but no one could agree how to pay - out of the rates or charging for the use of the engine? Four years later there was still no organised brigade and while the engine could throw water "its locomotive powers were impaired". It was not surprising to find that no accounts were kept and the vestry meeting was once again adjourned.

Country houses were isolated and vulnerable which is why lakes and water features were not just for recreation and ornament. On the 25 July 1835 The Times reported that the elegant mansion of Mrs Leake of Longford Hall near Newport, Salop was on the Friday accidentally set on fire in consequence of a servant employing herself in distilling water allowing the flames to overwhelm her. Engines from Lilleshall Hall and Newport were in speedy attendance and the flames were prevented from spreading to the main building though damage amounted to hundreds of pounds, thankfully insured.

Another fire occurred at Woodcote Hall on the outskirts of Newport in June 1874 when the house was empty except for the housekeeper and maid who discovered the fire at 4 o'clock on the Friday morning. A messenger galloped off to Newport whose engine arrived about an hour later, and soon after the engines from Weston Park, Aqualate and Lilleshall Hall. The gentry had longed learned to look after themselves when it came to fire protection. "For several hours (they) poured vast quantities of water on and into the burning mansion" and though much was rescued only the outside walls remained standing of the 1767 brick structure. Such tragedies were popular with sightseers who flocked to see the destruction and had to be controlled by policeman. Poor old Mr Cotes had only succeeded to the property five months earlier on the death of his father.

On the 8 November 1875 came the first meeting of a new local government body the Newport Salop Local Board which took over the responsibility for fire establishing a new brigade in June 1876 consisting of ten men stationed at the Royal Victoria Hotel with hose drying equipment. At first came simple improvements such as personnel returning their uniform when they left the brigade; people causing chimney fires to be fined 2/6; brigade to train once a month and have an annual trial on Easter Monday. By 1878 the brigade consisted of a Captain, Thomas Marsh, and firemen William Boughey, Edward Dawes, Henry Perry, William Weate, William Brown and George Ridgeway. Thomas Marsh was a plumber in High Street, William Boughey a saddler and harness maker in Lower Bar, Edward Dawes a milliner, William Brown a bricklayer in Beaumaris Lane and William Weate a builder.

By now there was a purpose built engine house at the side of the Market Hall though some were not happy with it. They also had 10 tunics at 12/- 8 pairs of leggings at 15/-, 2 pairs of boots at 28/-, 10 belts at 3/-, 4 axes at 4/-, 2 helmets at 15/-, 8 caps at 4/6, 3 driving lamps at 20/-, 3 searching lamps at 7/6 a total of £24.14.06d.

The charges for the brigade were free for ratepayers and £2 outside the parish with half fee for those Fire Offices (Insurance Companies) that contributed £1. For attendance at a fire the Captain received £1 and the men 5/- for the first hour and 1/- for every subsequent hour. The Captain received an annual payment of £6 and the men £1 dependent on attendance at drills and maintenance.

The real improvement in the fire service came in 1879 with the appointment of Mr Alfred Massey as Superintendent after the dismissal of the previous one for misconduct. He formed a brigade of eight retained men. As millwrights and hydraulic engineers the family had been around for years being involved with James Watt of Soho, Birmingham and Thomas Brassey the railway contractor on the Liverpool-Manchester line. Their hydraulic rams can still be found in the Newport countryside. At the same time the water supply was taken out of the hands of the Burgesses, who were dissolved, and placed at first with the new District Board and after 1894 with the new Urban District Council. By 1882 there was a well trained brigade with leather hoses replaced by canvas though no rescue ladders.

They were put to the test on Monday 28 March 1882 when Weale`s timber yard in Station Road set on fire, ironically it was about to be demolished to make the new road Granville Street. [Avenue]. The works were destroyed including all the workmens' tools and a subscription was raised to replace them. "In about half an hour the Fire Brigade arrived on the scene with the engine being fixed at a point in the Station Road.

Fortunately a fire plug was at hand and notwithstanding the fact the water had to be pumped 60-70 yards the engine, manned by a party of willing hands, was soon in action and a good supply of water was kept up". The Advertiser was asked by Captain Massey on behalf of the brigade to thank Mr Ward of the nearby Springfield Brewery "for his kindness in providing refreshment for the men on Monday evening".

They still had the old manual engine. They marched in Queen Victoria`s 1887 Jubilee procession: "Newport Fire engine and brigade brought up the rear: a grand sight, the engine being drawn by a magnificent black horse lent for the occasion by the L&NW Railway Co. The fine physique of the brigade in their accoutrements and their manly bearing, made a rare show, and they were much cheered as they marched along."

As the engine was now run by the local authority a scale of charges was issued in 1891:

For use of engine and equipment:-	£2.02.00 for the first 3 hours; 5/- for each hour after.
For services of brigade:-	£3 for first 3 hours; 14/- each hour after
For services of pumpers:-	£3.05.00 for first 3 hours; 14/- each hour after.
Superintendent:-	15/- and 2/6 for each hour after.
Horses:-	£1.01.00.
Driver:-	5/-
Postilion:-	5/-

To include cost of cleansing engine, hose etc but not the cost of damages.

In an interview in January 1897 a local fireman told the Newport Advertiser that they had a manual engine and a hose reel and could be ready in fifteen minutes being summoned by a bell except after 10 o'clock at night when they were fetched by a runner. All firemen could get up steam and drive the engine with two on duty each week and one attending the engine house every evening. There were weekly drills and no pay except for attendance at a fire when they received 1/- per hour.

"The Advertiser Almanack" for 1899 describes the Newport Brigade with Mr. A. Massey as Superintendent and Mr. W.M.Sillitoe, the caretaker of the Market Hall as his deputy. J.Heatley, J.Edwards, W.Heatley and J.Millward were firemen with H.Keeley, J.Cheadle and G.Boughey as Auxiliaries. If a fire occurred in the town notice had to be given to those who held the keys to the engine, that is Mr.Sillitoe at the Market Hall and any of the firemen. A fire outside the town, in the country, was a more elaborate routine, particularly if horses were required to pull the engine, then the messenger had first to give notice to the Royal Victoria Hotel and then to any of the firemen. The messenger was advised to shout "Fire" as he proceeded through the town. Before the engine arrived at the scene of the fire in the countryside a place had to be prepared for the engine to stand to enable the firemen to tackle the blaze as quickly as possible. Any person, boy or girl calling a fireman to the engine was rewarded. One fireman alleged, that as the youngest in the brigade his job was to go ahead and keep the fire going until the engine arrived! Perhaps he was not joking.

That year the Urban District Council refused to allow the engine to attend fires where neighbouring parishes and landowners had refused to subscribe though by 1900 Edgmond (£2.02.00) and Church Aston were paying. With a new water supply in the town the reservoir became redundant and was disconnected from the mains. Connecting the reservoir for a fire had meant that the ordinary water supply became contaminated for weeks.

The engine moved around different stations in these years at first in Middle Row then in 1878 accommodation was provided by the Market Company in their yard off St Marys Street, they also paid for the fire bell on top of the engine house. By 1905 it was based in Salters Lane at the Council Yard and stayed there until 1934 when it came back to premises in St Marys Street. From 1875 it was the custom for the Superintendent to be the surveyor, sanitary inspector and waterworks manager to the District Council, at first Alfred Massey, then followed over the years by Peter Darroch, John Adams and Reginald Charles Bryan (1941).

The most shocking incident since 1665 occurred in the early morning of 29 November 1910 when Aqualate Hall on the Stafford Road out of Newport overlooking the large mere, was burned down. There had been a fire at the Hall in May 1882 but thanks to the abundant water supply provided by the extensive water works of the local hydraulic engineer, Mr Massey, it was soon controlled with only £50 of damage. The 1808 house built for Sir John Boughey to the designs of John Nash was destroyed, only the original eastern part remaining today. Lady Boughey and her daughter Ethel Boughey, later Mrs Morris owner of the Hall, were in residence when servants discovered the fire in the library after 6.30 am. The domestic servants tackled the blaze with a hand pump while Ethel went back to her room until 9am only after then did she have the fire bell rung summoning the outdoor staff and sent for the Newport brigade. Staff then brought out the estate manual engine and the Newport manual engine arrived with a full complement of men at, so the newspaper reported, ten minutes past eight. Times vary with each account. This was described as "a remarkably sharp turnout." They concentrated on the eastern end manually cutting a gap in the roof to stop the spread of the fire. By this time all the gothic part of the building was alight and little was saved though many had flocked in including the usual roughs looking for adventure.

FIRE AT AQUALATE, 1910   OSBOURNE PHOTO

The "Eagle", the Eccleshall manual, arrived at ten o'clock and like the Newport engine laid on to two large water tanks in the stable yards which were kept supplied by a standing steam engine on the banks of the mere. The Wellington steamer having been alarmed at ten arrived at eleven o'clock "A remarkable fine piece of work, seeing they had to travel eleven miles." They were followed by the steamer engine from Stafford and both were used to relay water from the mere to the tanks where the manual engines did the actual fire fighting. There were delays; the Wellington hose burst, so they were still short of hose until the manual arrived from Stafford, only then was there sufficient to pump up the slope from the mere some hundreds of yards distant. Of the five fire engines only the three manual engines actually played on the flames and these stayed on duty all night as outbreaks continually occurred, the two steam engines leaving at 6 in the evening. The manuals did not leave until Tuesday.

Arthur Meadows (1891-1985) was an assistant at Brittain's grocery shop in the High Street and was one of the crowd who went down to see the fire. He recalled the manual engine had a bar each side to pump water from the mere, one of which he grabbed and helped to pump.

The stories and the post mortems began. The fire is said to have started in the vast old central heating system, the staff not daring to wake the household until 7.30 am then apologising for disturbing them! Crowds of sightseers were so vast that police were drafted in from Stone and gamekeepers put on the lodges to keep spectators out. Various Boughey male relatives motored over on the Wednesday and adjourned to the Royal Victoria Hotel where they "were all drunk as owls" and for Christmas poor Ethel was the only one left at Aqualate.

Ironically, at the time, the Newport Urban District Council was costing the purchase of a steam or motor engine and appealing to local parishes for help with finance. With the Aqualate fire in mind they met again but the old questions remained unresolved, who should pay for fires outside the district bearing in mind Newport had its own hydrants and volunteers and subscriptions; should the engine be motor or steam; should it be paid for out of the rates. Many parishes were reluctant to pay, some like Hinstock, had their own volunteers and engine which had been pulled by a horse, then a lorry until the new Traffic Act made this illegal. We do find the Newport engine attending fires at Hinstock in 1874 and 1922. The Hinstock engine was sold in the 1930`s for £2.50.

So nothing was done and things became ludicrous as in March 1921 when the Urban District Council decreed that because of the difficulty of finding horses anyone outside the district wanting the engine would have to send their own horse to pull it. There was another conference with neighbouring parishes in 1925 about a new appliance but the manual engine remained and had great difficulty in tackling fires outside the urban area so that the Council again in September 1926 ordered the brigade not to attend such incidents.

The Gallery - before and after the fire

The ruins of Aqualate

Before we become too horrified it appears that Newport Urban District Council was not alone in such actions, it was a policy adopted throughout the country. In a remarkable book "Small talk at Wreyland" written by a country gentleman, Cecil Torr, and first published in 1918, we find the same thing happening in Bovey Tracey a small town in Devon on the edge of Dartmoor. Bovey had a fire engine but no horses for it so the engine was not sent to fires. Like Newport this did not matter much to people living near the water mains as there was enough pressure for working with a stand pipe and hose and the fire brigade made their own way to the fire. People living further off were told on 6 April 1920 that the Parish Council felt it their duty to notify all or any person requiring the Fire Brigade with engine that they must take the responsibility of sending a pair of horses for the purpose of conveying the engine to and from the scene of the fire. Those knowing the very narrow lanes around the moors will not be surprised to know that even with horses the engine could manage only a funereal pace. It seems Newport was not exceptional.

By 1933 there was still no engine in Newport except the manual and for country fires they had to send for the Shifnal or Wellington brigades, Shifnal taking fifteen minutes to reach Newport. Newport did boast a ladder, but four members of the brigade were over 60 and six replacements needed to be found. They did purchase two hundred yards of hose to be kept at the fire station in St Marys Street and some uniforms and boots and fire extinguishers. The hose cart was kept at 9 St Marys Street with each fireman having a key though at one time hoses were kept at the firemen's home with a plaque over the door indicating "Fireman".

Motor traffic was now getting heavier on the A41 through Newport but the fire service could not cope, refusing in October 1936 to go to a lorry fire at Chetwynd Firs as being out of their district. It had to be dealt with by Market Drayton nine miles away while a similar incident on the Stafford road required Stafford brigade which was ten miles away. The newspaper had a scathing editorial saying the equipment in Newport was primitive and outside the range of the street hydrants the firemen were reduced to spectators. There was still a manual engine, some hose and an extension ladder while Wellington Urban and Wellington Rural councils had a joint motor engine.

Other technologies caused problems not envisaged by the old brigade as in June 1917 when fire broke out at 10-15 on a Saturday evening in the operating box of Wrights Picture House in the Town Hall, caused by the ignition of film. Walls were damaged and blackened, windows broken, floors scorched and doors blistered. The insurance claim was £23.16.06 and £2.15.00 to the Urban District Council for the fire brigade. Another fire occurred at the cinema in November 1921 in the entrance hall, the damage to equipment being over £400 which was not insured.

As if things could not get worse they did on a Sunday morning in November 1936 when fire broke out in the original 1665 building at Adams' Grammar School. Forty boarders were above the blaze which was discovered at 6.30 am and they filed out carrying a suit of clothes before returning to attack the fire with buckets of water. The seat of the fire was the staircase in the north-west wing where charring can still be seen. The caretaker who lived nearby alerted the police then ran to the fire station to sound the alarm but found the bell had stuck and refused to ring. The police sergeant had to cycle round and wake the brigade who eventually arrived at 7.10, forty minutes after the alarm. The caretaker meanwhile had found a length of hose connected it to a hydrant by Lloyds Bank in the High Street and had nearly reached the building when the brigade arrived. After an hour the fire was out. The headmaster quite reasonably was not amused and wrote protesting to the Urban District Council who agreed to provide electric warning bells in the houses of firemen.

At last in November 1937 the UDC provided £600 to buy a Pyrene trailer fire pump for £395, a fire escape, 100 yards of hose, 9 helmets, 2 respirators, 9 axes, 2 foam extinguishers and a uniform for the Fire Chief. Later they tested the new pump which threw a jet 80' high to the top of the church tower.

The fire brigade knew how to upset the right people, first the headmaster and in 1939 Dr Elkington, Newport's premier physician. He thanked them for saving his house in Upper Bar, next to Smallwood Lodge, but pointed out their deficiencies with a war coming, such as if the hydrants were put out of action there was not enough hose to reach other sources such as the canal. He asked for electric bells in the firemen's homes something which had been promised in 1936 but not carried out because of cost. The UDC did buy an extra length of hose.

The coming war focussed minds and already in 1936 the County Council coordinated all the local authorities and volunteers in one central ARP (Air Raid Precautions) scheme. In January 1939 an auxiliary brigade was formed with eleven volunteers and Bert Stanworth, the local undertaker, agreeing to haul the pump for a retaining fee of £3.03.00 plus 10/- (50p) per journey within the urban area.

Newport Fire Brigade WWII

In 1941 1,666 fire authorities were formed into the National Fire Service (NFS) consisting of 56 forces of which Shropshire was one. In 1948 the County became the fire authority inheriting, as in Newport's case, much worn out equipment and ancient buildings. By 1950 the service consisted mainly of part-time men and many resigned because of working conditions. Newport had eight men led by George Bartaby but it was estimated that at least thirty were needed plus a new station. A new station was opened in Salters Lane, Newport in 1958 replacing the one in the yard of the Royal Victoria Hotel and the siren, formerly on the police station, was moved from the church tower, because of the complaints of the congregation, to the Vine Vaults and then to Serck Audco where many of the retained firemen worked. Still there were moans at this reorganisation and that of the ambulance service, arguing that centralisation undermined the status and independence of the town. Such arguments are still used today. The amazing thing is that given the shocking history of fire prevention that Newport survived unscathed.

Duchess Blair.

The Sutherland children called her "Duchess Blair" a derogatory title reflecting their fear and hatred of someone they saw as a malevolent, manipulative confidence trickster. This was one of the many scandals of late Victorian Society a period which saw the greatest gap between the rich and the poor in English history, between wealth and poverty, which would have ended in revolution if the war of 1914-18 had not intervened, indeed in Ireland in 1916 and Russia in 1917 it did lead to revolution.

Caricature of
George Granville
3rd Duke of Sutherland

The dispute involved George Granville the 3rd Duke who had a mistress who for convenience we will call Mrs Blair, or Duchess Blair, throughout. When his wife died in 1888 he married Mrs Blair with undue haste and on his death in 1892 his will left his personal fortune, well over £1 million, to Mrs Blair and also some control over property, contents and the estate. Cromartie, the son and 4th Duke, his wife Millicent and his sister Alexandra, naturally contested a document which they believed had been drawn up under her malignant influence. On her part Mrs Blair, who like all the best confidence people, was well set up and presented, leaked long stories to the newspapers which would have done credit to the modern Sunday tabloids.

The Sutherlands were so rich in land if not in actual money that they were described as the "Leviathans of Wealth". It began with James Leveson (pronounced Luson) a wool merchant from Wolverhampton who did well in the speculation and purchase of monastic property during the dissolution by Henry VIII. He bought altogether about 30,000 acres including about 2,000 in Leegomery and Ketley, 6,000 in Trentham, 8,000 in Lilleshall, for which he paid £2,715, and 4,000 in Sheriffhales. Apart from a few mishaps, by the time of the industrial revolution they were in a position to exploit the wealth of their estates and were soon into mining and quarrying, furnaces and foundries and canals, helped by their choice of excellent partners and agents who were all important men in their own right - the Gilbert brothers, who were also agents to the Duke of Bridgewater, the Bishton brothers, ironmasters and James Loch. Income from industry was spent on improving their land with enclosure and drainage, new modern farms and roads particularly on the Weald Moors and in improving the lot of their workers, the estate providing houses, schools, hospitals, churches and clean water.

In 1785 George Granville Leveson Gower married Elizabeth, Countess of Sutherland, bringing in the vast Scottish estates and just before he died in 1833, the title of Duke of Sutherland with a monument on Lilleshall Hill. They also inherited the vast wealth of the Duke of Bridgewater of canal fame.

The 2nd Duke had a wife who used the money to build five great mansions including Trentham (£172,000), Dunrobin (£54,000), Stafford House in London and Cliveden in Buckinghamshire. Lilleshall Hall built in 1820 at a cost of about £80,000, was meant to be the home of the eldest son.

This then was the situation when the 3rd Duke, George Granville, inherited in 1862, a different man to his deaf and retiring father. An open air man who loved hunting and shooting, fires and fire engines, he, along with the Prince of Wales, had an agreement with the Metropolitan Fire Brigade to be alerted to any major fire so that they could go and watch! He also had a passion for railways, investing in Turkey and Egypt with his own private line and locomotives in Scotland so we have a Duke who drove his own engine on his own line burning his own coal. He was also a gambler with dubious morals and a member of "Society", the fast set surrounding the Prince of Wales and so frowned on by Queen Victoria.

He liked to be a bit of a radical, supporting the Liberals until Gladstone converted to Irish Home Rule and using his yacht to send supplies to Garibaldi, the Italian revolutionary, and bringing him to London and entertaining him at Stafford House surrounded by half a million people. On the other hand he entertained the Shah of Persia at Trentham who was far from a democrat. He accompanied the Prince of Wales to Egypt and India as a personal guest but invented an excuse to come home early.

If the Queen did not like the Duke, his wife Harriet was welcomed at Court where she was a lady in waiting and almost the Queen`s sole companion after the death of Albert. The job entailed endless tedium and it is not surprising that Duchess Harriet became religious and her marriage declined. When her husband became involved with Mrs Blair the Duchess refused to live at Trentham and went into seclusion in her house, Sutherland Towers in Torquay where she was visited by the Princess of Wales who had suffered similar infidelities with the Prince. She died there aged 59 in November 1888 and within three months the Duke had flouted convention and scandalised the family by whisking Mrs Blair off in his yacht to his property in Florida where he married her. She was 42 he was 61.

Mary Blair, Mary Caroline Mitchell, was the younger daughter of the Rev. Dr Mitchell, Principal of Hertford College, Oxford and was the widow of Captain Arthur Kindersley Blair of the 71st Highland Light Infantry who was shot and died from his wounds in a hunting accident in 1883 near Pitlochry. One story is that he was a dependant of the Duke and was accidentally shot by him. She was an imposing person describing herself as a "queenly figure", very tall and over twelve stone in weight. Others described her as a "grabber" with a violent temper. She was taken to Trentham while the Duchess was still alive shocking the family, the household and the village.

Of the others involved, Cromartie the 4th Duke married Millicent Fanny St Clair-Erskine, he was 41 and she only 17. Both were of a philanthropic bent towards their communities sometimes being over meddlesome. They built churches at Muxton, Granville and Donnington were anti-drink and very conscious of their social duties and position, the opposite of Mrs Blair. The daughter, and sister of Cromartie, was Alexandra who had trained as a nurse and sided with the sons against Mrs Blair. She died of rheumatic fever aged 25 in 1891. Whether it was the shock of the Blair case or not, Cromartie became increasingly concerned over money and began economies though they were not short by normal standards. They sold over 1,000 pictures, pulled down Trentham House in 1911, sold Stafford House and began the first of the sales of the Lilleshall estate in 1912. Cromartie died in 1913 but Millicent married several times and lived until 1955 still a prominent social figure.

Mrs Blair married the Duke in March 1889 and there appears to have been some reconciliation with Cromartie but this was all blown apart by the Duke's will when it became obvious that Mrs Blair despite her words of friendship had worked on the Duke to pass his money in bulk to her. The will was dated 4 August 1892 and a codicil was added hours before his death on the 21 September 1892. Mrs Blair knew well what the reaction from the family and the public would be and in June 1892 at Trentham she had prepared an apologia for her actions, that is before the will was drawn up and before the Duke's death. This she issued to the newspapers in December 1892, firstly the Glasgow Herald and then in the Newport Advertiser 3 December 1892.

The pamphlet consisted of ten closely printed pages with a preface explaining why her and the Duke had had to publish it. The preface says that the Duke and Mrs Blair had been advised to record the events of the last three years as regards the attitude of the children, that is Cromartie etc, towards them and that this true and faithful account would show how they had been forced into the sad quarrel between Lord Stafford, that is Cromartie, and themselves. The opening passage tells how she and the Duke became engaged in the middle of 1889 and that the marriage was to take place in the coming autumn. The Duke wrote to his three children to tell them this and asking that they received the new Duchess kindly and continue their affectionate relations with him. The answers were unkind and hostile to Mrs Blair and the Duke responded by persuading Mrs Blair to marry him at once, something she insisted she did not want to do "but the Dukes wishes were then as ever paramount." This is a justification she uses frequently, it was always the wish of the Duke and she as his wife, and out of her love for him, was bound to carry out those wishes.

At the end of April 1889 they returned to Stafford House to find that Lady Alexander had crated ornaments and removed them to a warehouse also all papers and documents including many letters of a sentimental nature. The same had happened at the Torquay house. Mrs Blair had previously written to the two sons and Lady Alex hoping they would come to like her and would visit but there were no answers and Alex continued to write "disagreeable" letters and did unfriendly things for example only meeting her father if Mrs Blair was not there. This said Mrs Blair caused talk and bad taste in the neighbourhood. Cromartie too, invited for a shooting holiday had used it to spend £200 on furniture leaving the bill for the Duke who did not mind, she said, as he was determined to promote friendly feelings. The pamphlet also alleges that Cromartie told them that his mother had given her blessing to the future marriage of Mrs Blair and the Duke and she professed astonishment when he denied it.

"Duchess Blair"

Mrs Blair raised another issue asking for Tittensor House near Trentham as a future dower house for herself knowing full well Cromartie and his family used it in conjunction with Lilleshall Hall. She then suggested that the Duke needed it for a short time because it was good for his health and alleged that Cromartie was telling people his family had been thrown out. In December 1892 she went to the Chancery Division of the High Court to restrain Cromartie from interfering with her possession of Tittensor. The judges were not impressed holding that though she had stayed there with her daughter, the costs of the house and the staff were borne by the new Duke, Cromartie, and they could find no lease, so though Mrs Blair could spend Christmas there she could only remove property belonging to her. The idea was dropped, instead Mrs Blair came up with the plan to use her money from the sale of her London home in developing property on the Scottish estate which she said would be of great benefit and bring money into the county. She needed the permission of Cromartie as the heir and when he refused, suspecting it was another devise to secure a dower house, she accused him of trying to thwart and annoy them and moved into the courts again to disentail the Scottish estates and deprive Cromartie of his inheritance. The quarrel thickened, there were more grievances about cutting down trees and paying the costs of Lady Alexandra`s death and the whole thing became painful and absurd.

The published extracts roused comment and indignation amongst those who had known Lady Alexandra and her charitable work or who had been the recipients of the charity of the new Duke and Duchess. Consequently, a representative of the Glasgow Herald went to Lilleshall Hall to interview Cromartie, who, declining details, made a few comments. The pamphlet was a tissue of lies, he said, especially as regards his sister Alex; his mother never left a message of any sort concerning the marriage of the Duke with Mrs Blair and he would continue to live at Lilleshall in a quiet way and do his duty to the estate.

Cromartie of course disputed the will and it was entered in the Probate Division. Meanwhile Duchess Blair commenced putting up rents in Longton, much of it the property of the Longton Corporation, for example the gasworks, being on ground leased from the Sutherlands. In return the new Duke continued Christmas gifts of beef and clothing to the locals and entertained the workforce to dinner and promised to increase the old hospitality.

The old Duke could not dispose of the settled estates or family heirlooms but his will gave almost all of his personal fortune to Duchess Blair or put it under her control. She received the maximum legal jointure of an annuity of £9,000 made up £5,000 from the English estates and £4,000 from the Scottish. He left a cash legacy of £100,000, upped before his death to £150,000, payable within twelve months of his death. She also got a lease of Tittensor for 21 years and the contents of Stafford House and Lilleshall including furniture and plate and drawings and a life interest in Florence colliery, Trentham, and other mining shares. She also got the disposal of the Sidway Estate near Stoke on Trent. Included also were any six carriages and any eight carriage horses of her choosing. The Duke also expressed a wish that Duchess Blair should have the use of the family diamonds during her life. More sinister was the condition that she should hold the residue of the estate in trust for her life merely asking that when she disposed of it she should show preference to the real heirs if they had treated her well during her widowhood. There was £12,000 for Miss Blair, annuities for servants and some furniture for Cromartie and Millicent.

As we have said Cromartie disputed the will but while the case was pending came a bizarre incident typical of Duchess Blair. A court order had been made for the inspection of certain documents in Stafford House. In the presence of both her own and Cromartie's solicitors she threw one of the documents on the fire alleging that it was a personal letter written to her by the Duke before their marriage. Legal proceedings were taken against her and on 18 April 1893 she was found guilty of contempt of court and sentenced to a £250 fine and six weeks imprisonment, her air of martyrdom rather offset by her luxurious arrival and departure from gaol. Immediately on her release she issued a glossy account of the incident through a carefully staged interview. It appeared in the Newport Advertiser on the 3 June 1893:

The report said the Dowager Duchess of Sutherland left Holloway gaol at 8.15 on Monday morning in a closed Victoria drawn by a pair of chestnut horses and attended by a footman. Her Grace who was attired in half mourning did not appear to have suffered any ill effects from her six week confinement. She was accompanied by a lady and a gentleman who arrived at the gaol with a portmanteau at 7.30 am. Her departure from prison was witnessed by a crowd of about 40 persons. She arrived home at the Willows, Windsor, at 12 o'clock and at 2 o'clock a deputation arrived intending to present a small token of their sympathy but the

Duchess Blair fatigued by her long road journey indicated she would see them later. Before leaving they left with her staff a solid silver casket on which was the inscription "This casket with £250 the amount of the fine imposed was presented on May 29th to Mary Caroline, Duchess of Sutherland by a number of English and Scottish friends as an expression of indignant protest against the severe order made by a judge for having unflinchingly carried out a dying request of her husband." Her brother asked the press to thank her friends who over the six weeks had sent her hundreds of letters and telegrams and presents of flowers. She had, he said, lost a lot of weight and had suffered acutely but was cheerful and hoped that rest and quiet would prevent a reaction and permanent injury to her health.

After her journey from Paddington station to Windsor, so much for the fatiguing road journey, she was interviewed by a lady journalist in a carefully staged setting. The welcome was quiet, two young girls with the party being greeted with a gentle smile by the Duchess and an affectionate embrace. A friendly parrot showed signs of delight at the return of its mistress and a couple of footmen bowed as she went through the picturesque hall. The interview took place in a shady nook of the garden with the Duchess in deep mourning having simply exchanged her black bonnet for a sailor hat. Her only ornament was a magnificent string of pearls looking more gleaming and beautiful against the "studied simplicity" of her costume.

The account described how she looked thin and her white hands twitched and there was pain and weariness on her face. She greeted the interviewer quietly and gently thanked her for coming to hear her side as all the papers, without exception, had published column after column criticising and condemning her. She agreed to tell the simple facts about the whole affair: "When the Duke lay on his deathbed in September last he said to me one afternoon in the presence of my brother, Mr Worthington and others, I want you to look up from my papers a certain bundle of letters and to destroy them all. You must search for them in London and our various country places until you find them and then burn them. The same evening, quite late, when I was all alone with my husband he talked about the letters again and said my darling you should do this for me and I know you will do it. Of course I promised and I meant to keep my promise. I should explain that these letters referred to a very, very grave, family scandal which happened many years before I came into the family and which the late Duke was anxious to suppress, so that no more trouble should arise from it for anybody."

The footman interrupted demanding whether her Grace would like her luncheon sooner than usual. "No thank you" the Duchess replied as the shadow of a smile flitted over her face at the tacit assumption that after the prison diet she would no doubt stand in need of a meal. "No thank you I am not at all hungry, we will have luncheon at the usual time." Then with a dreamy look at the lovely green world around her along a deserted, silent, river she went on, "all what has been said about the haste and hurry about the attempt to conceal the note I destroyed is absolutely and entirely untrue. Here are the facts; last March and please take note it was only in March that I was allowed to look through the late Duke`s papers, though he had died in September, we were searching for the bundle of letters which I had promised my darling husband to destroy. The letters could not be found but in my search for them I came upon another letter which lay somewhat crumpled under other papers. It looked, I noticed, as if it had stuck at the back of the drawer as letters sometimes do. I opened it, it was from the Duke of Sutherland to me before we were married, there had been a great number of letters for we had been engaged for nine months. I looked at it, there was nothing on the first page of especial interest but when I turned the next page I found something referring to the grave family scandal, not mind you the actual letter I was told to destroy but a letter referring to the scandal which I knew my husband would wish me to destroy.

After reading it I quietly folded it, put it beside me on the table and presently walked slowly across the room and put it on the fire. It is not true that I rushed across the room, I had a trailing dress for one thing which would have prevented me from running. And then I am not in the habit of doing things in a hurry. When those in the room saw what I was doing one man raised some slight protest and then for an hour and a half we went on working. It was only three days after that all this ridiculous fuss was made. What downright nonsense to say that I burnt papers relating to my dear husband`s will. Why that will is a heavy, bulky document and the letter I burnt was a sheet of notepaper. I see now, the Duchess went on presently with a sad look and a very low voice, I see now it would have been wiser to have not destroyed the letter. It could not harm me if it all were known for as I said before, it happened eight or nine years before I came into the family. Only I had promised my dear husband in his last hours to keep this scandal from coming up again and I would not have been the woman I am if I had not been faithful to his dying wish and for this reason I am glad I destroyed the letter though if I was more worldly wise I would not have done it."

She went on to describe her time in prison her doctor saying he had never seen before such a change in a person she having lost two stone. The loneliness was terrible with only three visitors a week, none of the prison rules being relaxed for her. Prison was made bearable by the thought she was doing what the dear Duke would have had her do. The journalist left with the Duchess Blair still playing nervously with her rings and protesting the truth.

Who can doubt from this article that she was the devoted, caring, loyal, innocent wife, suffering the outrageous calumny of her stepchildren because she had dared to love their father?

The date for the action over Tittensor was fixed for the 5 June 1893 but the main hearing was up for 7 June 1894 by which time a compromise had been reached. Though there are few public details it appears that Duchess Blair renounced the estate in return for a cash sum traditionally quoted as £750,000. In keeping with her character the cash was delivered in a sack in specially printed £1,000 denomination notes which when safely in her account were returned to the Bank of England to be burned. Her daughter, by 1912 the Countess Bubna divorced with two children, appears to have had the same propensity for cash for after her mother's death we find her claiming back £14,000 from the executors of her mother's will which had been given to her in cash but paid into the executors account by mistake. The Countess was already receiving £50,000.

Duchess Blair was still pursuing her aim to live on the Sutherland estate but Cromartie would not allow this so she had to be satisfied with building Carbisdale Castle just across the river from Sutherland territory. One account says that the Sutherland family agreed to build the castle as long as it was outside their lands in the old County of Ross and Cromarty, but others claim she built it out of her own inheritance cleverly locating it on a hillside, Carbisdale Heights, and visible to a large part of Sutherland and adjacent to the main road and the rail line which the Sutherland family would have to use to travel south. Duchess Blair employed a firm of Ayrshire builders and started work in 1906 producing a square tower with numerous extensions and different stonework to give the impression of age.

The clock tower had only three faces one remaining blank so that the Sutherlands when passing would not receive "the time of day". In return, it is said, the Duke would draw the blinds on that side of his carriage when he passed en route to his home at Dunrobin Castle. It became known locally as "Spite Castle" a malignant gesture to the Sutherlands.

Carbisdale - "Spite Castle

In 1933 the castle was bought by Colonel Theodore Salvesan a wealthy Scottish business man of Norwegian extraction and in World War II was used as a refuge for King Haakon VII and Crown Prince Olav of Norway. Harold Salvesen, the son of Theodore, gave the estate and the house to the Scottish Youth Hostel Association in June 1945 and it still serves this purpose.

It was unfinished at her death on 25 May 1912 aged 64 by which time she had married her third husband Sir Albert Rollitt MP. Her estate was £470,000 and she owned, as well as Carbisdale Castle, the Rawlins estate in Staffordshire and the Sutherland Manor estate in Florida. There were legacies to brothers and sisters as well as the £50,000 to her daughter and all her personal effects. She insisted on being buried in the Leveson-Gower mausoleum at Trentham.

Even when she was out of the news Duchess Blair could not avoid notoriety being robbed of £30,000 of jewellery when travelling with her third husband and servants in 1898 on the train from Paris to London. Of course it was no ordinary jewel thief but "Harry the Valet" the infamous William Johnson.

A remarkable insight into the character of the duchess comes in a letter from W.H.Russell the war correspondent of The Times, the man who revealed the horrors of the Crimean war. Dated 29 June 1896 it says "It really is true this time - the Duchess Blair is going to marry our friend Albert Rollitt! Which of the two is most to be pitied - which rather most deserves the other, and the dreadful fate that is in store for him or her!"

Mrs Keppel the mistress of Edward VII said of marriage and men "never do anything for nothing and not much for sixpence"; Duchess Blair was of the same ilk a really careful, calculating, ruthless operator.

The Marked Man.

An entry in the log book of Newport National School on 8 July 1904 reads "I William Carr, head master of this school determined my engagement here today". Commenting, the Newport Advertiser which was a liberal and nonconformist journal had no doubts about the reason, Mr Carr, it said, was a marked man and it was because of his liberalism that he had had to leave. To them he was a martyr. What had he done? He had caned a boy but there was nothing unusual in that then or later; twenty five years on another Newport head spread eagled a boy over a desk, had two men hold him down, flogged him in public, was exonerated, compensated and became a minister in the Church of England. Thirty years later a head at the junior [National] school caned fourteen boys at once for tapping on a neighbour`s window on the way to school. He remained as head for thirty years. What was the difference? What was so special in the case of William Carr? The difference was that here was a young, radical man, determined to do something about the terrible condition of his pupils in a conservative town.

One reason lies in the voluntary and religious nature of the school, built as a result of the 1870 Education Act which decreed that if you do not build your own school you would have one forced on you, paid for out of a compulsory rate and managed by an elected Board, hence a Board School. Newport not liking rates, then or now, went down the voluntary path, built a school out of subscriptions so that it was always short of money and consequently good teachers some of whom were little older than the children they taught. Underfunded, overcrowded with a generation of children who had never experienced the discipline of education or simple things like turning up, sitting down and responding to time. Elementary education, national, then compulsory and only lastly, free, was a new experience for everyone.

The school opened on Thursday 20 March 1873 the first headmaster being James Keeley from Smethwick who trained at Saltley Training College (Birmingham). In his first year he formed a drum and fife band, took children on excursions by train to the Wrekin and other treats and games and teas, even so the average attendance was only 300 out of a possible 500 children. Mr Keeley was superintendent of the Sunday school, which was held in the schoolroom and had more pupils than the day school, was secretary of the choral society, a sergeant in the Rifle Corps and collected the Gas Company accounts. He died in November 1889 aged 47.

William Threlfall Carr was born in Galgate just south of Lancaster and was trained at Chester College. He came to Newport to cover during the illness of Mr Keeley and took over when he died in 1889. He was only 23. This young man was faced with immense problems the first two being finance and attendance. Though attendance was compulsory and Newport had its own Attendance Committee to enforce it, education was not free. In 1889 when Mr Carr took over, the school fee, often referred to as the school pence, was 3d a week bringing in about £90 pa. There was a government grant determined by attendance and those pupils passing the annual tests, the rest came from subscriptions - a man being paid to raise such funds - church collections and sales of work. Every year there was a deficit. Some were proud that while other schools spent £2.01.08 per pupil on education, Newport spent £1.10.06 the cheapest in the district and they were not pleased when Mr Carr pointed out that this was nothing to boast about.

As for attendance there were rules and fines for non-compliance but the Attendance Committee were often unwilling to convict poor parents and were quite willing for children to leave for employment when below age because this relieved the poor rates and many of the committee were Poor Law Guardians. Many members secretly agreed that children above the age of ten were better off employed rather than being educated. Mr Carr fought this committee publicly and in the press for years and this lost him many influential friends.

He had numerous battles with local employers who needed the cheap labour as much as parents needed the extra wage. In 1890 he complained bitterly about parents keeping children at home for frivolous reasons such as running errands which took a whole day and could have been done after school. Many children continued to leave early even though not beneficially employed and having reached the required standard to obtain a "labour certificate" allowing them to work. Farmers and landowners flouted the regulations at harvest and at shoots and if the Attendance Committee did not act he often approached employers directly, threatening them until the children returned to school. Mr Macklin the fishmonger was one in 1897. Absenteeism meant lower school income and lower teachers salaries and less respect for teachers though Mr Carr fought his case on purely educational grounds. In the question of child employment Mr Carr had the moral ground but sympathy lay elsewhere, with the poor who resented being forced to school and forced to pay!

Another frustration was the leisurely approach to schooling connived at by all sections of the community, which revealed itself in the enormous number of holidays, days, and half-days which interrupted lessons. There were days off for every church event whether C of E, Catholic, Methodist, or Wesleyan, Sunday School sports, trips, choirs, no matter, they all reciprocated; there were events at other schools such as the Grammar School or Merevale; there were town events like the Flower Show, the May Fair, elections and visiting circuses. To oppose these entrenched interests did not make you popular.

By far the greatest cause of absence was illness often epidemics of whooping cough, measles, mumps, scarlet fever which led to weeks of closure and frequent deaths. Closure and isolation were the main remedies and the whole situation was compounded by malnutrition and dirt.

Another cause of disruption was lateness the reason often economic with children being kept back to do jobs before going to school. In 1902 he had had enough and refused entry to any child coming to school after prayers.

There were problems with staff particularly pupil teachers often girls as young as seventeen supervising classes of 50 pupils while the older assistant teachers not only had to be supervised but also tutored to get them through examinations. Employing unqualified teachers was self-defeating because as the standard of teaching went down so did the government grant.

By the time of Mr Carr the buildings and fittings were thirty years old and while there had never been enough money for revenue there was certainly never enough for maintenance, replacement and improvements. Very little beyond painting had been undertaken while the front wall needed rebuilding as did the girls toilets and the playground was unusable the children in very wet periods, having to play in Avenue Road. Spouts and drains were acting as ventilators for the sewers. In such an environment no wonder he was stressed and disillusioned, children could not read, spell, add or subtract or take an interest in life despite the introduction of music and maypole dancing, observation, walks, prizes and a local museum; education was bottom of the list for children who came to school dirty, diseased, hungry and unclothed.

Mr. Carr and pupils

Mr Carr was a reformer and had high hopes of change but nothing was straightforward the introduction of free education in 1890 simply brought overcrowding and space was so short the schoolroom at the Congregational Church had to be used until a new Infant block was constructed in 1898. He had similar hopes for the 1902 Education Act which took schools away from the church and into the hands of the Local Education Authority, Shropshire County Council, but they too had little money and even cut the school budget while the new managing body found itself still responsible for the fabric of the building as its predecessors had done. On a personal note Mr Carr now found himself having to pay a rent as well as the rates and taxes on his school house on a salary of £147 pa. The school was now so crowded that there was space only for desks and certainly no room for internal exercise or assembly.

Mr Carr had always been a supporter of Board Schools which he felt had a larger and more reliable income from the rates and who could therefore have better premises, facilities and teachers and could develop and experiment. He was the first secretary of the first local branch of the National Union of Teachers and at meetings of managers and teachers he not only favourably compared Board Schools to voluntary schools but supported equal pay for women teachers when local clergy opposed the idea on the grounds that women could not guarantee continuous service. For this reason they would not employ married women. These views would hardly have endeared him to his employers.

He was radical and reforming in other ways speaking frequently in support of Old Age Pensions which were introduced in 1908. He was a member of the Fountain of Peace Lodge of the local Manchester Unity of Oddfellows Friendly Society and Grand Master in 1895. He persuaded the Lodge to invest its funds in housing for members. The Lodge purchased Hen Meadow, across the road from the school, off the Marsh Trust for £250 and erected ten substantial houses. He wrote an article advocating his views on housing called "My own landlord" which was circulated worldwide and these houses are a memorial to his work and ideals. He was not only an officer of the Lodge but enjoyed the social life with meetings based at the Pheasant and Smoking Concerts at the Town Hall. He was young and active and he was soon on the committee of the Choral Society taking the principle tenor solos in concerts and a member of the cricket club.

The Avenue Road Oddfellow Houses

71

In 1892 he married Miss Fife, a girl from Lancaster and we have to remember he was still only 26 and in three years had built up a substantial life in the town so much so that the Newport Church bells were rung three times to welcome them back from their honeymoon. Mrs Carr soon became well known and well liked, gifted with musical abilities and a rich, beautiful voice. In December 1898 she died aged 32 leaving four children the eldest only six. Two months later the eldest child was dead the school log book simply recording "I was away on Monday owing to the death of my child". So to the stress of the job was added the strain of personal tragedy.

Before we look at the 1904 caning incident, we must understand the major change in educational organisation after 1902, both elementary and secondary. Education was placed under the authority of elected bodies in our case Shropshire County Council. As we have seen Mr Carr was in favour of such a state system of education and immediately began to lobby the new officers but the county was huge, faced with a backlog of deficient buildings, poor staff, no money and enormous poverty in the rural areas and the market towns. There was not going to be a revolution in education. At home the new managers consisted of four from the church with the Rector as permanent chairman, two from the County Council and one from the Urban District Council, uncertain of their role and powers but anxious to do the right thing.

The annual report on the school in May 1904 by the Head and the school inspector paints a bleak picture for the newcomers. The school, it said, had been conducted with skill and energy and the work was deemed fairly satisfactory "under the conditions". These "conditions" were too large classes, too much dependence on pupil teachers, lack of qualified assistants, unsuitable desks and other deficiencies in equipment. The boys' cloakrooms were insufficient and the playground needed draining. The inspector hesitated in recommending payment of the government grant. The headmaster retorted that he had told the authority this several times and far from helping they had actually cut his requisition as they had the year before. He drew diagrams in the log book showing how overcrowded the classrooms were, classrooms ironically named Lilliput, Utopia, Arcadia and Olympus. The head's room was Elysium! To disappointment and frustration was added friction.

People in Newport seventy years later could remember the headmaster of the Junior School being "sacked" for caning a boy even if they could not remember his name; the story had entered folklore. There is no mention of the incident in the school log book though it is confirmed in the managers` minute book in the County Archives. In November 1903 the managers dealt with a complaint about ill treatment by pupil teachers and the Head and though they felt the complaint was unjustified they did warn Mr Carr that only he should inflict corporal punishment, not junior teachers.

On 7 March 1904 it was reported that William Thomas Rogers had been severely beaten by the Head and the injuries were inspected by four managers: "The Chairman reported that a complaint had been made to him on the previous Wednesday morning, by Mrs Rogers, of the ill treatment of her son William Thomas Rogers by Mr Carr. The boy was seen by 4 managers viz Dr Elkington, Messrs Brown and Smallman and the Chairman all of whom were unanimously of the opinion that he had been severely beaten. Mr Rogers applied for a common summons but on the evening was induced by Mr Carr to withdraw it." A letter was read from the father (4 March 1904) which simply said that Mr Carr had apologised and begged Mr Rogers to withdraw the summons to which Mr Rogers had agreed.

Dr Kitchen and Police Inspector Darbyshire also inspected the boy`s hand and felt the punishment had been excessive, given this and the fact that Mr Carr had been reprimanded in 1901 and 1903 the managers asked for an explanation. Mr Carr could only comment that he had no idea of the severity of the punishment until he saw the boy`s hand the next morning. The managers felt this was not good enough and he was asked to send in his resignation. Mr Carr rejected this and maintained that the boy was not injured and was attending school and he appealed to the County Education Authority. Such a case was the last thing the new Local Education Authority [LEA] wanted and they set up a committee of enquiry which met in the Marsh Trust Room of the Town Hall on 24 March. Here Mr Carr revealed that he had the chance of another appointment and, given his young family, he needed to accept quickly. He even asked the managers for a testimonial.

Privately the LEA had suggested to Mr Carr that he resign, which he did, while the managers withdrew their application for dismissal. As a result the County Council sub-committee never reported. There were rumours that LEA had offered Mr Carr another job if he would resign but in the end they compromised, they told the managers they had acted correctly while allowing Mr Carr to stay in the teaching profession which his years of service and record merited. His testimonial is therefore very carefully worded: "Mr Carr Head Teacher of the Newport National Schools having tendered his resignation to the managers his resignation having been accepted by them the managers beg to state that Mr Carr has for the past 15 years held the post of Head Teacher of the Newport, Salop, National Schools, during which time the successive reports of HM and Diocesan Inspectors have borne testimony to the efficiency of the school and the grants earned have been very satisfactory. The Managers wish Mr Carr every success in his future career".

He left to take up an appointment under the London Educational Authority with a clock presented to him by the teachers and pupils and a testimonial and a purse of gold from the Shropshire branch of the National Union of Teachers for his work as secretary.

To the editor of the Newport Advertiser Mr Carr was a martyr who had been forced out of his job because of his radical ideas; "....he was a marked man and for his liberalism he had to leave the school."

One pupil remembered his school, with its slate pencils and toilets with no deep drainage, a wonderful master with no favourites, and also his advice to leavers "When you go out into the world you will find many things that you have not seen in Newport. But whatever you see or hear keep within the folds of your bible and the knowledge you have learnt." They remembered under him the science, the museum, the maypole dancing, the walks and the building of the new infant department in 1898; light where there had been darkness.

His successor Joseph Spencer Lawton criticised the alarming deficiencies left him by Mr Carr but as the years passed we find him too with the same deep seated social problems faced by Mr Carr, and his log book in turn echoes the sadness and frustration of that radical, educational idealist William Threlfall Carr.

In October 1914 William Carr writes from Salisbury Plain where he is waiting as a sergeant gunner in the Royal Field Artillery to go to France. His son David was with him. He asked to be remembered to all his former pupils. He died in London in December 1921 leaving a widow and family. He was, his obituary says, highly respected and much regret was felt when he left Newport.

There were lighter moments. In the Daily Graphic of 21 May 1896 Mr Carr was photographed with his invention of a new type of bicycle that had the rider seated inside a larger wheel pedalling a smaller wheel that rotated the outer. The inner cycle was, like a tank, moving along its own track, which, given the appalling roads at the time was not a bad idea. There was another report in the July edition of "The English Mechanic and World of Science" where he describes his invention as a unicycle, claiming a great saving of energy, a speed of 30 mph and easy mounting and dismounting. It would have required great leg strength to get uphill even greater leg strength downhill as there were no brakes and there were no pneumatic tyres. Mr Carr had several advantages; there was a company in Newport at the time, the Underhills, producing bicycles; the bicycle was still in its experimental age and he was a renowned mathematician who gloried in trigonometry so that his invention is a concoction of angles and circles and hypercycloidal curves. It does not appear to have hit the market. In losing Mr Carr, Newport lost not just a teacher but a man of ideas and invention.

Mr. Carr with his invention – May 1896

A Funeral and Four Weddings.

The name Rylands comes from the earth, from the cultivation of the soil. It could simply mean the land where the rye grows and certainly in earlier times the light soils of North Shropshire grew mainly rye. It depicts a type of farming just as the "Wheatland" is used to define South Shropshire. "Ry" or "rea" or "ria" can be a river and water and the derivation could imply "land by a river".

Crossing the marshes north of Newport and through the gap between the Scaur and Puleston Hill where Chetwynd Manor is carefully sited and the River Meese escapes from the "Mere Eye" through dense reeds and plant beds, you enter a land of gentle slopes and placid streams. Here the "Sleepy" Meese is joined by equally peaceful streams the Lonco Brook, Ellerton Brook and the Wagg before flowing on to the river Tern and eventually the Severn at Atcham. This is a landscape formed out of the Bunter and Keuper sandstone themselves a prolific source of water with light, blow-away soils and an average rainfall of 26 inches a year, an area specifically suited to arable, livestock and dairy farming, including the famous Cheshire Cheese.

The nature of the land lends itself to large estates, large tenant farms and large fields. Over the years, arable and dairying have given way to sugar beet, then oilseed rape and now the agri-business of pigs, poultry and potatoes. A countryside of isolated farms and small hamlets such as Puleston (Pilson), Pickstock, Chetwynd, Howle, Ellerton, Weston Jones and Loynton, it was here that the Rylands family flourished for over nine generations first at Loynton and Norbury, then Puleston and Calvington with Newport as the hub of their activities.

The earliest Rylands was Radulphus a husbandman or farmer of Loynton in the parish of Norbury, he died in 1599. Thomas, his son from his first marriage, was born in 1553 and moved later to Puleston, to the household of George Salte. Whatever his status when he went to Puleston, at his death in 1598 aged 43, he was a bachelor described as a "yeoman". He was the first Rylands to be buried at Chetwynd. He was joined by his sister Margery and then his half-brother John, it was John who continued the line. In the inventory of Thomas we find twenty sheep worth £2.13.04 (£2.67), cash at £3, wearing apparel assessed at 50p and a small coffer at 5p. He was not rich but neither was he poor. They were the tenants of

Lord Kilmorey formerly the Needham family who had the land from the Chetwynds and later sold to Richard Bayley of Standford Hall; from here it passed to the Bayley Marsh's, a widow of whom married the Rev. William Dalton and at her death Puleston and much more was bought in 1864 by J.C.B.Borough who was extending the estate quite cheaply at the time. Col. Borough, the last Borough, died in 1960 and between then and 1987 the land was sold piecemeal mainly to tenants.

An inventory of 1619 included three cows, a heifer, one mare, one hogg, eight geese and six hens; in the house were brass, pewter and wooden items, four chests, three bedsteads and all the testators apparel; in the yard, muck or compost, corn and hay.

Robert, the second son of John, continued at Puleston followed by his two sons Robert and John. Robert (1648-1722) began the custom of marrying into similar local families creating a network that lasted until the twentieth century. In 1675 he married Mary Bayley a member of the Edgmond family whose name survives in the name "Bayley Hills". It was their eldest daughter Mary who married into the Adams family of Tibberton and Edgmond in 1709. They had a son Thomas Adams who in 1750 married another Mary Rylands of the next generation, they being first cousins.

We know that Robert Rylands (1685-1748) had eight children and as a "yeoman of Pilson" though not wealthy had enough to live on and left copyhold estates in Lapley and Wheaton to his eldest son John and all the stock and implements at Puleston to his second son also Robert. The third son Thomas and his sisters including Mary (Adams) and Sarah (Bailey/Bayley) were left sums of money. John died without issue aged 33 and the brothers Robert and Thomas continued at Puleston. Father Robert and sons Robert and Thomas were all churchwardens and buried at Chetwynd.

In 1784 the brothers helped form the Edgmond Association for the Prosecution of Felons along with several other notable names such as Pigott and Bayley. This suggests they were well-off to support such a commitment. The Chester Road (A41) was a known haunt of highwaymen and rustlers.

Robert died childless and Thomas the third brother continued the line with his wife Anne Wild of Pickstock. Their son, also Thomas, for it had now become the custom to name the eldest son such, married Jane

Sillitoe of Forton Hall in 1798 while his sister Elizabeth married Thomas Blakemore of Newport, substantial merchants and bankers who by the 1820s described themselves as "gentlemen". There is a plaque in St Nicholas' church which reads: "In an adjacent vault are interred the remains of Elizabeth Blakemore who was born 3rd October 1763 and who died 2nd September 1828, wife of Thomas Blakemore, gentleman of this town, and daughter of Thomas Rylands, gentleman, and Ann his wife. Also of the above named Thomas Blakemore who died 15th March 1833." The connection continued for in 1878 T.S.Rylands acted as executor to John Blakemore a farmer of Edgmond who left £14,000.

This Thomas died in 1848 and was buried in the graveyard of the old Chetwynd church behind the Hall, to be followed shortly by his 13 year old granddaughter, Charlotte Jane, one of the eight children of Thomas and Elizabeth. The vault and the inscription are still there though for over one hundred years, through a dispute with the Borough's, the family were unable to visit the site.

Son Thomas (1799-1870) took over from his father in 1841, probably two farms as well as other fields on the Dalton estate. This Thomas married Elizabeth Masefield of Ellerton from Banshee the large house in the Forton Road, Newport, now the Rylands nursing home. This way the property came down through the Masefield family in to the possession of the Rylands. Thomas and Elizabeth retired to Banshee where she died in 1866 and he in 1870 being then a director of the Market Company. He left an estate just under £18,000.

Thomas' will, drawn up in 1865 and proved in 1870 was a substantial document. By this time there was a different farmhouse probably Puleston House the present farmhouse on the Pickstock Road. All the household furniture, plate, glass, linen, books, wine, fuel and other household goods, and the horses and carriages went to his wife though she predeceased him. Thomas Samuel was left the tenant right to the farm, the contents and livestock, including oxen, and equipment such as winnowing and threshing machines, wagons, carts, wains, carriages and the harness and saddles, vast wealth compared to the inventories of 1598 and 1619. His elder daughter, Elizabeth, received a legacy of £8,000 and financial provision was made for his younger daughter, Emily, who married Robert Taylor Masefield, of Ellerton Hall. They too were first cousins.

Banshee provided a wider social life. The new market hall of 1860 had a large assembly room which became the venue for important social occasions. The Annual Ball had dancing from 10.30 till 4am, a huge menu, followed by a hunt. Patronised by the gentry, Sutherlands, Cotes, Boughey, Leeke and Borough it was a must for "respectable" families like the Rylands set. In February 1862 the company included the Rylands, Heanes, Liddles, Masefields and others. Emily Rylands opened the dancing. The Ball was something of a marriage market.

Things were now beginning to change. After years of pressure a new bridge had been built over the Meese at Puleston in 1812 with a straight road replacing the original which started to the right of the present Garden House, and crossed the river by a ford nearer the Hall and on up to the base of Puleston Hill and then turned sharp left under the hill towards Pickstock. Here under the hill were the original Rylands farm, Puleston Hill Farm, with buildings and a small settlement including a blacksmith's shop and cottages. This farm was taken down around 1850 and replaced with Whitley Manor Farm. The settlement, including the blacksmith's which is still there, moved to the present junction. The original road is now a green lane under the hill. Mabel Wheat in 1954 said that the pump and a copper beech still remained of the original settlement. The pump at least is still visible on the corner of the green lane and the present road.

Original road and site of the Rylands' Farm

Another disturbance was caused by the decision of the Burton Boroughs to close the old church next to the Hall and build a unified group of church, rectory and school at the junction of the Chetwynd and Edgmond roads, the present site. No doubt there were good reasons; the need for a school to accommodate the changes in elementary education after 1870; a more convenient site; the old church was inadequate for those attending; but it is suggested that the real reason was that the old church interfered with the privacy of the family at the Hall. Being good churchmen the Rylands assisted in the construction by transporting building material as they had with the building of Sambrook church.

The churchyard was now closed officially and the Boroughs refused access to the Pigott and Ryland families to their family vaults and to future burials. The Borough family could be quite eccentric and John Charles Burton Borough disputed the assignment of pews in the new church, hid the key to the chancel, put his servants in the choir stalls guarded by a policeman, and interfered with the running of the church by the Rector, the Rev. F.C.Young, whom he forced to leave.

A more dramatic event around 1866-68 was the purchase of the Puleston land by the neighbouring Burton Boroughs. This, combined with the problems of access to the old churchyard, seemed to have unsettled Thomas who had been at Puleston all his life. In 1866 he handed over to his son Thomas Samuel Rylands and died in 1870. After nine generations the Rylands determined to leave Puleston for Calvington in Edgmond parish. It could of course be that Calvington appeared a better prospect.

Thomas Samuel Rylands (1839-90) was father and grandfather to the last generations of Rylands and the last to farm. Christened at the old Chetwynd church, which he served for many years, he was always irritated by the fact that he was not allowed to be buried there. He farmed for his father at Puleston until 1866 at which point his mother had died. His diary records how at the age of 26 he began to farm on his own account and altered the farm buildings. He lists the profits for the first four years as £477 in 1866, £240, £278 and then £317 in 1869 when he became engaged to Alice Edleston. He went to live at Puleston in 1868 and left in March 1870. He took Calvington on Lady Day 1872 and moved in there in August 1873. He had property in eight areas of Newport, including two farms, though he did not farm himself.

Calvington was rented from the Morris Eyton family who still own the property. The Morris family were solicitors in the eighteenth century and came to Newport dealing with the affairs of the Baldwyns of Aqualate Hall. Calvington was originally in the hands of the Yonge family who sold to William Briscoe in 1763. Having borrowed money from the Morris family the farm was put up for sale in 1829, did not sell, and in 1837 Charles Morris agreed to purchase for £16,714. From here it came down through a younger branch of the family.

Thomas and Alice farmed at Calvington for eighteen years and had a family of six children, two sons and four daughters; it is his funeral and the weddings of his four daughters that is the reason for this story. When Thomas Samuel died on 14 November 1890 he was a gentleman of substance, all his farming stock live and dead, household furniture and goods and his personal effects were left on trust to a value of £17,696. But what was extraordinary was the manner of his death during a performance in the Lyceum Theatre, London at the age of fifty in front of the actor Henry Irving no less.

A report in the Newport Advertiser on 22 November describes the profoundly painful impression that was felt in the town when the rumour of his death spread by word of mouth, so unexpected that it was hoped, like other rumours, it might prove untrue. A report in The Times the next morning confirmed the worst fears. He had with Mrs Rylands and his eldest daughter gone to London and was staying at the Langton Hotel. On the Friday evening they visited The Lyceum where "Ravenswood" was being performed and at the close of the third act Mr Rylands fell forward. Two doctors in the audience attended and he was carried out but was already dead. Mr Irving who was also manager of the theatre placed a private room at the disposal of the family. An autopsy revealed heart disease. The body was brought back to Newport on the Monday night and the funeral took place on the Wednesday.

The funeral at St Peter's Church, Edgmond, was impressive, attended by mourners of all ranks. Muffled peals rang out all day and the hearse was followed by six carriages from the Victoria Hotel with estate workers as bearers. Among the many wreaths was a special one from Henry Irving made up of camellias and chrysanthemums, roses, orchids and fern. A large Celtic cross was erected in St Peter's churchyard where he had served so long.

The grave of Thomas Samual Rylands

His death brought to an end the centuries of farming by the Rylands, his wife and daughters going to live at Park House, Chetwynd End, Newport. In 1893 his widow Alice married Sidney Pennington a Professor of Veterinary Science a family friend but much younger that her, the daughters being left to the care of their Aunt Elizabeth at Banshee. It was she who launched them into marriage for marriage was the only career such girls were going to have and it had to be marriage into their confined social group, to men who could afford their life style. This meant late marriage as potential husbands had to wait until they had succeeded to the family business or had forged a new career for themselves.

The eldest daughter Alice Elizabeth of Park House, Newport, known as "Lillie", was married on 30 August 1898 aged 27 at Christchurch, Lancaster Gate, London to William Fortescue Clayton of London, son of W.G.R.Clayton of Broughton, Manchester. The marriage was conducted by the Rev.Preb. Burges, Rector of Newport, and she was given away by her uncle Colonel Masefield. The bride wore a dress of silver grey poplin trimmed with white satin and pink chiffon with a white hat trimmed with feathers and pink carnations. She wore a pearl and turquoise brooch the gift of the groom and carried a shower bouquet of pink carnations and heather. Her mother, Mrs Pennington, wore a dress of dove-coloured bengaline silk trimmed with white satin and lace while her mother-in-law, Mrs Clayton had a dress of petunia brocade. Her aunt Elizabeth wore a dress black silk canvas over heliotrope silk and bonnet to match. As might have been expected the most gifts came from the aunt, with silver, silver sugar tongs, diamond brooch, worked centre piece for the table, cookery book, prayer book, silver Indian necklace and a silver cigarette case. Relations present were all in the social network, Deringtons, Elliott, Masefield, Liddle, Heane, Burges and Hodges. The cake was supplied by Messrs Buzzard of Oxford Street.

The next daughter was Gertrude Chambers Ryland the second daughter aged twenty two. She married Rowland Pemberton Liddle the third son in the legal dynasty. Aged 27 Liddle was ready for a wife having recently become a partner with his father and sole owner when his father died in 1900 and amalgamating with rival firm Heane in 1903 to create Liddle and Heane. He was a formidable character and struck terror into Newport until his death in 1959 aged 84. The wedding at St Nicholas church was a major public occasion with a large congregation of guests and public and decorations and displays at Hurlstone (the home of the Deringtons), Chetwynd House (Elliott's), Rosemont and archways at Banshee and garlands in the grounds. The church was decorated by the Misses Derington.

The young bride wore a dress of ivory white duchess satin flounced with accordion pleated chiffon draped with old Limerick lace. The groom presented her with a pearl and diamond necklace. The bride was given away by her mother. As the bridal party left the church children from the Girls Home at Edgmond strewed flowers in their path. The reception was held at Banshee the home of Aunt Elizabeth.

That now left the twins Alice Maud (Birdie) and Julia Frances (Bunny) born in 1882. Alice Maud aged 27 married first in 1909 to Harry Percy Rogers of High Onn near Stafford the son of Harry Rogers of Bickford Grange, Penkridge. The bride who was given away by her brother Harry Randal Rylands, was dressed in cream Japanese glace with embroidered panels of irises and water lilies; she wore a tuile [Tulle] veil over a wreath of real white heather and carried a bouquet of white heather and white carnations. Her twin sister Julia and her nieces Ileene Clayton and Margery Liddle were bridesmaids. The dresses of the bride and bridesmaids were made locally by G.H.Sidebotham later Plants. It was a very public occasion with a large congregation in St Nicholas church which had been adorned with palms, plants and flowers, for a choral service, and bunting lined the way down Forton Road to the reception at Banshee. This time the cake was made by the Newport confectioners Anne Elkes and Sons with three tiers with vase and bouquet streamers, each tier being supported by silver pillars and the silver stand was encircled with a wreath. A remarkable photograph of the cake by John Brown of Newport has recently been discovered. There was a huge collection of presents from everyone of note in the neighbourhood including Sir George and Lady Boughey.

The fourth bride "Bunny" Rylands in 1911 went from Banshee to Forton Church. She was 29 and married Arnold Lawrence of Ellerton Hall. Her little nephew Charles Rylands Liddle was page boy. Ellerton Hall a large red brick building was built on the site of a previous house by Robert Masefield one of a family who lived there until 1906 when Colonel R.T.Masefield sold the estate to Colonel Lawrence. Arnold was his son and was noted in 1911 as being the chief landowner. He and Julia lived there in some style until 1954.

Just over a year later on 2 May 1912 Aunt Elizabeth, Elizabeth Ann Rylands, died at Banshee aged 80 and was buried at Forton. The top end of Forton Road was then in Forton parish and Staffordshire. Described as a forbidding lady to look at, she had made her spacious house a home for her brother's children and launched them into adulthood. Her obituary said she had been unwell for some time but even so the death cast quite a gloom over the village where she had won the affection and respect of all who knew her and who had been ever willing to extend a helping hand to those in need. The sale at Banshee in January 1913 was over two days with Elkes doing the catering for a modest charge, in a large marquee. The house contained a dining room, drawing and breakfast rooms, kitchens and eight bedrooms. The outside effects included a brougham, four wheeled pony carriage, dairy cow, poultry and a stack of hay. The total value of the estate was given as £11,010. Banshee was left to her two nephews.

J. Brown,

PHOTO OF

Wedding Cake

SUPPLIED BY A. ELKES & SONS,
ON THE OCCASION OF THE MARRIAGE OF

Miss A. M. Rylands and R. P. Rogers, Esq.

NEWPORT, SALOP.

Banshee
Now Rylands' Nursing Home

The four brides had two brothers, Thomas Edleston Rylands, born 1872 and Harry Randal Rylands born 1878 both described as tall, good looking men. Boys at this level did not attend Adams' Grammar School, Tom going to Malborough and Harry to Shrewsbury. Unable or unwilling to go into farming both sought careers abroad, Tom in Burma and Randal, having gained a diploma at the Royal Indian Engineering College, on the installation of the telegraph service in India. The Empire was a job creation scheme for boys of such families the Novaportian Club handbook of 1914 out of a list of 213 former pupils at Adams' Grammar School had 28 working in the colonies, 13%.

Randall Rylands married Dorothy Budgen daughter of the Rev Budgen another family in the clan. They lived at the former girls home called

Moorfield in Edgmond the same home that had scattered flowers at his sister's wedding.

Tom at his death in April 1947 was described as one of the most picturesque personalities in the life of Newport. He served with the Bechuanaland Border Police and was taken prisoner in 1896 during the Jameson Raid. Subsequently he worked for the Bombay and Burma Trading Company and was a superintendent of teak and timber in Burma returning home in 1911. He then worked for Whittinghams builders and timber merchants in Granville Avenue and Station Road. In 1914 -18 he rose to the rank of Captain in Home Defence and commanded a POW camp on the Isle of Man and in the second war was in the ARP. He became an Urban District Councillor one of the famous "twelve apostles" all alleged to have been nominated by the Newport Bowling Club, six of whom were elected in 1925. They maintained they were not a clique or a party but simply sought "progress" using slogans and large adverts like "A fair field and no favours" and "Progress with economy". As late as May 1930 the whole council and officials toured the town and ended at the bowling green where all were members. He stood down in 1946.

Captain Rylands had wide interests, as well as the Bowling Club, where he served as president. He was a director of the Market Company, the Literary Institute, Cricket Club and was a keen sportsman with big game hunting and fly fishing. Not surprisingly he married late, aged 45, in 1917 to Hilda Heane daughter of R.N.Heane who died in 1944. Their son Lieutenant Michael Rylands was wounded in Normandy in 1944 and was later ordained in Chester Cathedral in 1947. Captain Rylands had extensive property under the Rylands Trust including lock-up shops at 87 and 89/91 High Street and land extending down to Beaumaris Road with workmen's cottages. They lived in New Street and their garden, which is now New Street car park, had tennis courts and a summerhouse.

The Jameson Raid took place on 29 December 1895 one of those Imperial adventures that still afflict British politicians today. Dr Storr Jameson of the British South Africa Company led a force of 470 mounted men with maxim guns and a field gun from Bechuanaland into the Transvaal to support a supposed rebellion of foreign workers in the gold fields of Johannesberg. The conspiracy failed and led eventually to the Boer War of 1899-1902. Tom Rylands, described as a tall, athletic young gentleman, back home in Park House, Newport, gave an account of the invasion and his part in it, with music and slides, at a lecture in

Wolverhampton. He was, he said, serving in the Bechuanaland Police and had not the faintest idea when setting out from Mafeking as to where he was going and it was not until they crossed the border that he realised where he was bound for. As a trooper in the Mounted Police he had only a few days before being transferred to the Chartered South Africa Company and this did not arouse his suspicions. He described cutting the telephone wires and the first shot he heard in the middle of the night when he was asleep on his horse as he and many others had been for many miles travelling at a walking pace. It was too dark to do much shooting. Cyclists brought orders from the British authorities to return immediately but at the battle of Doornkop the raiders were finally surrounded by the Boers. "There the bullets" he said "began to come like hail and men and horses to drop. I lost my best chum there. He was shot through the heart so did not suffer much pain. He had my coat on at the time and was buried in it". After being engaged for three hours and most of the day and night before, with little food and sleep - half a tin of sardines and Scotch - someone put a white shirt on a long stick and ended the affair. The firing stopped and they were surrounded. He was close to Jameson at the surrender and they were escorted to Pretoria as prisoners and then to England. Jameson was imprisoned in England but returned to Cape Colony and became Prime Minister in 1904.

Today there is not a Rylands in Newport or any of the exclusive, self contained network of clergy, lawyers, doctors, gentlemen farmers and Officers, respectable, well-off professionals, not quite gentry but serving the gentry, that set the style and fashion in the Edwardian days of Newport.

The Milliner's Tale.

On Monday at Birmingham Assizes, before Mr Justice Kennedy, Mrs Julia Howle of the Square, High Street, Newport, Salop brought an action against Arthur Hulton Harrop of Lythwood Hall, Shrewsbury for damages for the betrayal of her daughter, Gertrude. So ran the newspaper report of April 1904 which was to reveal a multitude of Julia`s problems ranging from drink, sex, seduction, deception, bankruptcy and scandal involving the four highly respectable families of Maddox, Howle, Ashmore and Harrop. This was the Edwardian age of middleclass morality when everything was covered over, women by high-necked long dresses, even table legs allegedly wore curtains, and revelation led to disgrace and exile. In reality, as today, everyone revelled in the sensationalism, and in a small town like Newport all knew what was going on.

Who were the characters in this drama? Julia Howles was Miss Julia Maddox milliner and draper of this town; her father was Thomas Maddox the proprietor of the Theatre Royal in Shrewsbury as well as three shops and the "Shakespeare Vaults"; her husband was William Howle a photographer; her sister and brother-in-law, Isaac Ashmore, were the owners of Rosemont commercial school in Chetwynd End; Arthur Hulton-Harrop was a son of William Edward Hulton-Harrop of Lythwood Hall, Shrewsbury and a student at Harper Adams` Agricultural College.

Julia Martha Maddox, known as Cissie, the third daughter of Thomas Maddox, at the age of 22 had a fancy drapers shop at 41 High Street called the "Bon Marche". In 1881 she was living with her sister and brother-in-law, at Rosemont School. She was 28 and he 34 when she married William Howle in December 1884 and by 1891 they were living at 69 High Street where she continued as a draper and he a photographer and where a century later all the Howle glass negatives were discovered. At that time Gertrude was 5 years old.

William Howle was the son of Henry Howle one of the most talented townsmen of his day with palette and brush as well as the camera. His photographs of Newport are rare but his cabinet portraits and carte de visite can still be found while his pictures of working women are in the A.J.Munby collection at Trinity College, Cambridge. There is also a set of photographs of the outstanding trees on the Aqualate estate in the 1860's. When Henry died in 1889 William inherited the business and his talent but he also had another talent as a singer in huge demand in the town and beyond. We find him in Mr Smart's Annual Concert at the Town Hall in 1882 singing a long forgotten popular "serious" ballad "Ehren on the Rhine" where a soldier says goodbye to his love declaiming "My life is o'er, we'll meet no more"! In January 1885 after his marriage to Julia Maddox he is presented with a marble mantle clock by his friends in recognition of the way he had helped many causes with his "excellent vocal abilities."

But there was a flaw in his character he had what is usually known as a drink problem culminating in November 1902 in an incident at the Pheasant Inn with two other men when they were found, on two visits by the police, helplessly drunk, lying on the bar floor, incapable of crawling home even with the aid of a wall. They maintained they had stayed late to hear Howle sing and recite. They were charged with being drunk on licensed premises Howle being described as the well known singer and a man very quiet when sober. In fact Howle never turned up at court where they were fined 10/- [50p]. The landlord was fined £5 and 8/- costs and quitted the Pheasant soon after. Howle left the family home and at the time of the court case in 1904 Mrs Howle was said to have been separated from her husband for three years. In July 1905 John Brown another local photographer took over the Howle negatives.

At the Assizes Mr Stanger KC appeared for Mrs Howle and Mr Hugo Young for the defence. The defendant pleaded that he did not betray Gertrude and denied that she was the servant of her mother, the plaintiff. Mr Stanger said the claim was for damages for seduction and that charge was grave enough but made more painful and sad because at the time in question Gertrude was only 17 years of age and had only recently left school. The action was not directly for the seduction but for the loss of service and was brought by those, father, mother or employer who had lost the services of the seduced. It was therefore necessary to prove that the person seduced was in the service of the plaintiff and in consequence of the seduction the plaintiff had lost that service. So the case was not a moral one but an economic one. Only when they had proved the economic consequences of the case was it possible to go on and consider the pain and dishonour of the girl's seduction whereby the damages would be greater.

90

The young lady was living at home with her mother helping with the housework and in the business of milliners and fancy drapers. Owing to certain differences with her husband which she could explain, Mrs Howle had not lived with her husband for three years though he contributed in some small degree to the household expenses. Gertrude was the oldest of the children and the only daughter and on the 1 January 1903 she had attained the age of 17 and left school in May that year. She had shown considerable proficiency not only in playing the piano but also in singing and it was the object of Mrs Howle to develop her daughters talents and have her trained and with that in view Gertrude had gone to school in Lewisham High Road, London and had passed examinations connected with the Royal Academy of Music. She had become the protégé of the Duchess of Sutherland and Lady Boughey and a successful if not brilliant career in music was in front of her.

When she left school at Lewisham she helped her mother and pursued her studies to attain a scholarship to enter the Royal Academy of Music. At Lewisham she had been described by the headmistress and teachers as a perfectly modest, pure-minded girl, sweet and unsophisticated and an affectionate daughter. That was May but by August she was ruined and that condition had been brought about by the defendant.

Turning to the defendant Arthur Harrop, Mr Stanger said the only excuse that could be made was that he was young but his conduct since the complaint had not been exemplary. He was a student at Harper Adams` Agricultural College and had a bicycle which allowed him to ride into Newport though students had to be back in college by 9.30pm. He met Miss Howle and her brother at the Newport May Fair on the 28 May and then about six times afterwards. Her mother did not approve but she had no reason to believe otherwise than he was a gentleman. At the college was a farm bailiff by the name of Jones whose housekeeper, a Miss Davies, acted as the intermediary carrying letters, taking messages and arranging assignations. After a holiday one such meeting was arranged on 6 August and the next day after drinks in Edgmond, Getrude, her little brother and Miss Davies walked back to Cheney Hill at 8 o`clock where Harrop was waiting.

What happened then was Miss Davies and the little boy walked on and Miss Howle and Harrop, still pushing his bicycle, turned right, up one of the lanes off Cheney Hill where there were few houses and no traffic. He placed his bicycle against the hedge acted improperly towards the girl and forcibly took advantage of her. He told her if there was anything wrong he would take her to the doctor and when she cried and threatened to tell her mother he asked her not to do so. In fact she did not tell her mother being in such a distressed state that she gave the excuse of toothache. Three days later she met him by accident told him of the situation and he told her to take a bath in Condys Fluid and that he would take her to see a doctor. A week later she repeated her request to him to see a doctor an appointment she kept but he did not. She wrote to him, received no answer, and had not seen him since.

Cheney Hill, Edgmond

Nothing came to her mother's knowledge for three to four weeks and when she did find out Mrs Howle was very anxious to keep it from the public and hoped the matter might be arranged without a public scandal. The situation seriously damaged any chance of entering the Royal Academy of Music one condition being the entrant had to have perfectly good health. Though letters of recommendation had gone in from the Duchess of Sutherland and Lady Boughey and examination dates arranged the girl was unable to appear. Mrs Howle wrote to Mrs Harrop and received no reply then to Mr Harrop, defendants father, in which she said her daughter had been ruined and disgraced and further that she was sick and in a half-dying state. The letter concluded with a request that Mr Harrop should pay £500 compensation as it was a criminal matter; she said if Arthur Harrop had been of age she would have insisted that he married her. There was no allegation that Harrop had promised marriage just a half joke that they should run away.

Mr Harrop did reply asking for copies of any notes his son had sent to Gertrude. Mrs Howle did this. He then wrote saying his son denied the allegations. This prompted a reply from Gertrude to Mr Harrop saying that if his son did not behave as a gentleman she would follow him to the ends of the earth. She wrote: "I thought he had gone mad, he said he was madly in love with me and there were such things as runaway matches. He has ruined my character and prospects for life. My character was pure until I knew your son."

The cross examination of Gertrude took a familiar pattern; was she certain she had been seduced? Harrop had not seen her on that date; she had met or seen several other men who were named; she had been up the lanes with students at night; she had been seen by the police "gaming" with students; she had misbehaved on holiday by dancing on the sands; that the idea of getting rid of the baby was her own. The police were questioned as to why if they were concerned she was in moral danger they had not informed her mother? They said it was not their job. They also admitted they were willing to help Mr Harrop as he was a magistrate.

The attitude of Arthur Harrop was that he had not been there that night and this was supported by the evidence of his student friend and the daughters of Doctor Pooler of Old Hall who said he was with them playing tennis that night. The judge and the defence showed surprise when Mr Harrop could not recall what his son`s attitude was when he faced him with the allegation. Did he deny it or not, he was asked? Mr Harrop, said he denied it sufficiently and "in part". Arthur simply denied it in court.

In 1906 William Edward Hulton-Harrop is listed at Lythwood Hall, Shrewsbury, DL and JP., with estates in Lancashire, Shropshire, Flintshire and Yorkshire having assumed the additional surname of Harrop by Royal License. Deputy Lieutenant, High Sheriff, County Councillor and MFH; Conservative and Churchman with four other sons and two daughters, he was a formidable opponent.

It mattered little, the judge finding for the plaintiff with £1,000 and costs which did not preclude an affiliation order. Nevertheless because of the scandal Julia Howle felt obliged to sell up and move to Birmingham where at Sparkhill police court on 13 June 1904, Arthur Harrop was ordered to pay 5/- per week towards the maintenance of the child and solicitors and doctors expenses of £2.02.00 and £5.10.00.

Rosemont, Chetwynd End

This should have been enough trauma for one family but it was not, for Julia had a sister Emma Elizabeth who was married to Isaac Ashmore the highly respected head of firstly Chetwynd church school for seventeen years and then from 1884 Rosemont the private commercial school at the junction of the Forton and Whitchurch Roads. Frederick Howle, the brother who accompanied Gertrude on her trips up Cheney Hill was at the school. That same year 1901 Isaac Ashmore brought in his brother in law Mr T Maddox and his wife formerly Miss Frood of Merevale College. A branch of the school was opened at Ivydene for girl boarders. By 1906 he was in trouble and all the girls were transferred to Ivydene as a separate establishment calling itself briefly Newport Girls High School. Isaac was already handling the debts of Julia Howle and in July was faced with the death of his wife. Now aged 59 he employed a Miss Nangle as housekeeper and matron and later married her. The school was losing

94

money and in a desperate move he settled the furniture on his new wife to avoid creditors even though he knew he was insolvent. On the 21 January 1910 he was bankrupt, the school at Ivydene closed and the Maddox`s sold their furniture and left the district like their sister Julia.

The problem was not just the school but his involvement with the affairs of the family of his first wife. Isaac`s father in law was Thomas Maddox who died in September 1890 and he was the proprietor of the Theatre Royal in Shrewsbury as well as three shops and the Shakespeare Vaults next door. In 1901 Isaac took over the affairs of the theatre with another brother in law as manager. Between £7-8,000 was spent on improvements. In 1902 it was purchased for £10,000 mainly on mortgage by six Newport men including Ashmore and the solicitor H.G.U.Elliott, calling themselves "The Shrewsbury New Theatre Royal Syndicate." Ashmore was the lessee but he knew nothing about the business, depended on managers and lost money from the start. Shares had to be assigned to the County Bank to cover an overdraft of £1,300. Despite this the theatre actually survived until 1945 when it closed down through fire.

At the bankruptcy hearing Isaac Ashmore revealed that pupil numbers were down and the school was making a loss of £100 annually. He admitted that he kept no accounts and was "foolish" to take over the theatre through the persuasion of his wife and brother in law. By 1911 everything had gone and Isaac took a school at Weston Rhyn where he died aged 67 in 1914.

There was a happier note in May 1911 when Gertrude married Tom Harrison from Barnsley at St Patricks in Birmingham and in 1918, when William Howle died in Birmingham aged 68 back in the bosom of his wife, daughter and three sons.

The End of the Gentry.

Some years ago historians argued in learned journals as to whether in the Sixteenth Century the "gentry" were "rising or falling" that is were they increasing in numbers, wealth and political power or were they declining? Like all generalisations it is a pointless theory as social mobility varies as much by luck, chance, and ineptitude as much as by merit. The Lancashire saying "clogs to clogs in three generations" could apply at any social level. It certainly could be applied to three of Newport`s neighbouring landed estates.

Who were these gentry? They were, or are, a class or group below the rank of nobility, possessed of land, of certain manners and breeding which allows them to identify each other and be readily recognised by others. The country house and its occupants with their extended families, jobs, servants and ownership of land reflected a secure social order aided, in most cases, by a touch of nostalgia.

For generations they were the unpaid administrators in the countryside and even after the invention of County Councils in 1888 they provided the bulk of the councillors, the Leekes, Burton Boroughs and Bougheys all being County Councillors while Sir Thomas Boughey was Chairman of Newport Urban District Council after 1894.

Until 1971 they had judicial responsibilities as magistrates, until 1906 Justices of the Peace having to have property qualifications. Younger members of the families provided the local clergy as at Forton and Longford and built the churches. As well as the formal duties of their rank they customarily provided houses, schools, as at Chetwynd and Forton, and roads. The Sutherlands provided the water supply for Lilleshall and Donnington and the Leeke estate Newport's water. They chaired the Poor Law Guardians and dispensed patronage and pensions and the community rituals such as fox hunting, like the Albrighton Hounds, and beagles. They supplied the manpower of the armed forces and the law. They were never shy of dabbling in industry or commerce or of marrying money from whatever source.

The estates bordering Newport were, west of the town, the Lilleshall estate of the Duke of Sutherland which began with the dissolution of the monasteries under Henry VIII; to the south, the Woodcote estate of the

Cotes family who fought under Henry VII; the Longford estate to the west, Chetwynd estate to the north and finally the Aqualate estate on the Staffordshire border. Lilleshall and Woodcote went by 1914-18 finished by the war and the long agricultural depression; the other three of later origin lingered on, Longford into the 1930`s, Chetwynd until the 1980`s, with only a very truncated Aqualate with its hall and deer park existing today. (2010).

Longford, Chetwynd and Aqualate all came from new wealth generated by the industrial and agricultural changes around 1800, wealth used to buy land from older, declining families, Longford from the Earls of Shrewsbury, Chetwynd from the Pigotts and Aqualate from the Baldwyns. This was new wealth looking for landed status, the Leeke`s acquiring their wealth in India, the Borrow or "Boroughs" from commercial property in Derby, and the Boughey`s from industry and banking in Stoke on Trent.

The Leekes were an old Shropshire family appearing in Ludlow in 1334, marrying into the Mydlletons of Chirk Castle, the Ottleys of Pitchford and achieving high office under the Commonwealth. They were resident at the Vineyard in Wellington and were burgesses and High Stewards of Newport in 1714 and 1763. However younger sons had to make their own way and in 1780 Thomas Leeke of Wellington gave Ralph, his second son, £400 to take him to India following a path trodden by Robert Clive of Market Drayton. Clive returned a hero and a millionaire but most were swallowed up by disease or absorbed in the Indian culture.

From 1780 to 1785 Ralph was paymaster of Islamhabad and Resident at Tipperah under the Company known as the "Honourable East India Company". In 1786 he asked the Governor if he could return to England and came to live at Haughton near Shifnal and began to look for a wife and an estate to match his fortune. We know that on the 10 December 1787 a settlement of £10,000 was made on the marriage of Ralph Leeke to Honoria Francis Thursby, daughter of Walter Harvey Thursby of Shrewsbury, the money being used by Ralph as security for the Longford property. The Longford estate was valued in 1788 and in March 1789 purchased from Charles, Earl of Shrewsbury, nephew of the former earl who had died in July 1787 without issue or will. The house and land cost £40,125.

Ralph began the life of a country gentleman and between 1794 and 1797 was involved in considerable expense rebuilding Longford Hall to a very personal design of J Bonomi. The original hall had faced west and was now turned through a right angle to face south with a ha-ha separating the park. It was constructed of square stone blocks with seven by four bays, two storeys high with giant pilasters and a heavy porte-cochere of four large Tuscan columns and a pediment designed to keep the weather off those alighting from carriages.

Inside the entrance hall was a design from the Parthenon in Athens, a large bronze stairway and a lantern roof with, in plaster, the Leeke coat of arms and the Leeke logo of a "leg".

Longford Hall

Ralph removed the last remains of the Domesday village to enhance the view of the new Longford church built in 1806 by John Cobb of Newport. A large picturesque lake of 6.5 acres was constructed fed by streams from neighbouring estates. Similar improvements were being carried out at the same time at Attingham Park and at Aqualate. He even purloined stone destined for the new church to build new lodges leading to the Hall, the church that provided younger sons with a living for most of the century.

Ralph took his place in the social life of the town becoming a burgess and High Steward in 1812. Along with other prominent gentlemen he took the lead in raising the Newport Volunteers in 1803 drilling them on his fields, laying up their colours in Longford Hall and acting as commandant with the rank of Lieutenant Colonel. We find him using the Red Lion in Newport to carry portmanteaux and boxes to London and Cheshire by coach and for the carriage of pheasants, hares and other game as far as Birmingham and London. He frequently hired a chaise and horse for local journeys, as did his daughter at £6 per month, for social visits to local country houses at Aqualate, Woodcote and Shifnal. He was related to the Cotes and Pigott families. He was a member of the Coffee Room at the Lion with its oysters and newspapers and held his rent days there with the customary dinner and ale.

Though Longford was not a large estate Ralph had used his new wealth to secure his landed status and his position in the community by the time of his death in 1829. His son Thomas and grandson Ralph Merrick Leeke both had poor health and were absent from Longford for long periods the Hall being rented out. Though the family consolidated land and had interests in lime pits and brickworks it lacked the industrial base of its neighbour at Lilleshall. The family continued to do the things expected of local gentry - going to Harrow and Oxford, commissions in the army and navy, providing the local clergy and church, and filling public offices as Lord Lieutenants and magistrates and later councillors. They rode, they hunted, they shot and had servants, including a chauffeur, until the 1940's.

The last of the family, Colonel Ralph Leeke was born on Christmas Day 1849. In 1870 he purchased an Ensigncy and Lieutenancy in the Grenadier Guards one of the last to be able to do this. His brother followed the traditional path into the living at Longford church while a third son was drowned aged 26, in peculiar circumstances. In August 1883 Henry Leeke RN went ashore in West Africa to deal with a native dispute and on a shooting, sporting trip, with the ship's doctor, their boat was attacked and overturned by a hippopotamus and even though he was a strong swimmer, he was trampled by the hippo. He is buried at Church Aston.

Colonel Leeke succeeded in 1882 and lived at Aston Hall in the village of Church Aston, originally the Dower House. Longford Hall was rented out in 1883 to Daniel Adamson the promoter of the Manchester Ship Canal and between 1903 and 1935 to Colonel Sykes. Col. Ralph Leeke was to be the last of the Leeke family and with his death came the end of the Longford estate even though he had two sons Ralph Henry born in1883 and Charles born in 1887. The army was the career path of sons of the minor gentry and in 1902 we find Ralph then 19 doing the social rounds of the country houses drinking tea and playing bridge before joining his regiment in Cairo. The 1914-18 war was unkind to the gentry, it was brutal to Colonel Leeke both sons being killed, both unmarried. Major Ralph Leeke joined the Rifle Brigade in 1902 and by 1910 was serving with the 4th battalion of the Kings Africa Rifles in north east Uganda fighting against tribesmen. A few months after the war started he was sent to East Africa in charge of four companies of his battalion to fight the Germans. Here on 5 November 1915 he died of blackwater fever.

Charles Leeke like his illustrious predecessor, Ralph, sought his fortune in the Empire going to Ceylon in 1905 working in tea and rubber. The climate did not suit his health and he moved to British Columbia and was involved in trapping and mining claims. When war broke out he joined the Canadian infantry and later was a Lieutenant in the Grenadier Guards his father`s old regiment. He was with the British Expeditionary Force in 1914 and in August 1915 was posted to a machine gun company a unit that always received special attention from the enemy. He died of wounds on 11 April 1916. In May 1923 the east window in Longford church was erected in their memory by their mother. It is now in a corner of Newport church.

In 1935 and 1937 the estate was sold and stripped of timber by speculators, cattle drifting in and out of the Hall. During the war the army left the Hall in a shocking state removing all the steel and brass Georgian grates, the brass door handles but fortunately not the mahogany doors. The woods along the road and down the drive were cut down and the drive gates and walls smashed by the guns and tanks that were stored there.

The adults of the family lived on to great ages as if to compensate for the early, tragic, deaths of the children. Colonel Leeke died aged 93 at Church Aston in 1943 and was buried at Longford without flowers or music, like his sons, in the gloom and despair of war. His wife, also aged 93 died in 1947 and Miss Hester Leeke of Edgmond died aged 100 in 1949. A sister of Colonel Leeke she was the last of nine children and hunted the fox, the hare and the otter to the end of her life. With her a chapter ended; in four generations the line and the estate had gone.

The Chetwynd estate lies across the fields from Longford and like Longford sits on Newport's doorstep. The house stands on meadowland at the confluence of the river Meese and the Lonco Brook overshadowed by the high rock of the Scaur. For eleven generations the Pigott family had ebbed and flowed like the Meese, prone to lost causes like Charles l, the Jacobites and lastly the French Revolution. The decline was assisted by the gambling of Robert Pigott who died in France in 1794. The ghost of Madame Pigott can still be seen about Chetwynd Pool depending on the weather and the amount of ale consumed at the Three Horseshoes. The estate passed through several investors being offered for sale three times between July 1801 and May 1802 before being sold by private treaty. It then contained about 1,670 acres.

The purchaser in 1803 was Thomas Borrow of Derby a barrister whose wealth came from industry and property as Derby expanded and the railways came in. There are still streets in Derby reflecting the family names, Hulland Street, Chetwynd Street and Borough Walk. Barristers, recorders, mayors and sheriffs they already had the Hulland Estate which they held to the end, but were looking for another landed investment for their commercial capital.

The Borrows were absorbed in the running, the improvement and consolidation of their land. The first Thomas Borrow was by inclination a practical man, fond of mechanical work and his workshops, as was his grandson, John Sydney Burton Borough whose hobby was engineering and whose biographical entry read "chiefly interested in mechanical pursuits". He had a fine blacksmithing shop repairing all the machinery and later the tractors at Chetwynd. Over the century they created a integrated estate yard of brick, tile and iron with an estate office, a schoolroom, stockyards and foldyards, sawmill, metalwork shop, cowsheds, barns and a laundry at first driven by water, then steam and soon oil engines linked to bellows and grinding mills. Luckily residential development has retained all these working units.

They bought land often small copyhold plots scattered in the old open fields. Between 1825 and 1886 they obtained almost the whole of Sambrook a distinct village community with its own shops, craftsmen, post office and public house. By 1866 they had most of Puleston, Standford and in 1875, Pickstock. By 1907 they had 507 acres in Edgmond including the Lamb Inn. In 1883 they had over 7,000 acres,

5,000 at Chetwynd. They also inherited and unified the Castlefield and Hulland estates in Derbyshire.

A eulogy of 1889 described the changes of the previous thirty years with the estate extended, the land more fertile, fenced and drained; where there was once common land grew splendid crops; where there were once hovels splendid farmhouses and cottages. There were churches and schools, straight roads and bridges. Even in the hard times tenants in trouble were found work on the estate.

Chetwynd Park

Introverted and even eccentric compared to other local gentry the Borrows had their passions one being education and from the beginning they had a school on the home farm and schools at Chetwynd End, then Chetwynd and Sambrook and were instrumental in providing funds for Newport Junior School in 1873. It is proper that their name should continue in the Burton Borough School.

The last "Squire" was Colonel John George Burton Borough and when he took over from his father in 1924 the estate had become a limited company but with falling prices and falling rents farms were put out to the Watson Jones` and there was little investment or modernisation. The four years from 1948 to 1951 show, after deducting the Colonel's directors fee, only small profits on the estate and in 1949 a loss. Such profits were a most inadequate return on the total capital in the estate made worse by the habit of paying dividends to shareholders, mainly the family, well above earnings. The Estate was advised at that rate there would be no surplus left in a few years. Added to this was the problem of the Colonel's age from the point of view of potential death duties which would have meant half the value of the estate, and from his ability to administer such a responsibility. An agent could not have been afforded. In these circumstances the only way was for the Company to be liquidated and the Estate sold and the proceeds invested to leave the family in reasonable comfort with a reasonable income.

Another burden in 1951 was the big house with some rooms derelict and all needing repair at a cost of £5,000, a sum not justified given the financial position of the Company. Moreover it lacked all modern facilities, was too large for Col. and Mrs Borough and could not be staffed in those "servantless times". Negotiations for demolition and rebuilding went on for several years until the present house was constructed in 1964.

Time was bought with the sale of 1,475 acres in the north of the estate in 1953 and when the Colonel died childless in 1960 his estate was scarcely 3.000 acres. As he died without issue, despite a late marriage, for the last twenty eight years the estate was administered by trustees of Charterhouse and Christ Church to whom the bulk of the estate had been left. When Mrs Borough died in April 1987 the sale realised £3.5 million.

And so the Borrows, gentrified as the "Burton Borough`s", disappeared reluctantly but inevitably, after four generations, the Hall was demolished and the deer park with the original deer brought down from Derby, preserved by the Newport Agricultural Society. Today only the deer look down on what was once a unique, working, self-sufficient Victorian enterprise.

The deer and the park are still at Aqualate as is the house at the end of a drive sweeping along a glacial ridge providing an astonishing view of a glacial mere over a mile in length and half a mile wide, the largest sheet of water in Staffordshire. A wonderful setting for a newly created young gentleman for this is what John Fenton Fletcher was, a deliberate invention. The Fletchers, the Fentons and the Bougheys were all connected, bankers and businessmen in Stoke on Trent, while George Boughey was the last of four brothers, two lawyers, an apothecary and a clergyman, who all died childless. In their young cousin John Fletcher they sought to achieve their ambition to create a family of country gentlemen.

Aqualate Hall and Deer Park

The legacy was invested in trustees to purchase land which they did in 1797 buying Aqualate for £64,728 from the bankrupt Baldwyns. John came of age in 1805 adopting the Boughey name and coat of arms, marrying in 1808 and succeeding to his father's baronetcy in 1812. Between those years the Hall was enlarged and remodelled and the park redesigned by names like John Nash, Repton and Haycock.

Over sixteen years John produced nine sons and four daughters and family life dominated though he held public offices and was an MP. He died in 1823 of a fever caught from one of his sons. He was only 39 and with him ended any political or social aspirations the family may have had and they settled to being worthy squires. This early death meant that Thomas Fenton Fletcher Boughey the third baronet succeeded when he was only fourteen and as he lived until 1880 there was a continuity which allowed the estate to consolidate and prosper during the long Victorian golden age of agriculture. He was an improving landowner and at his death the estate covered 36 square miles. He fulfilled his civic obligations paving the streets of Newport and building new markets. He had twelve children.

Thomas Fletcher Boughey, the fourth baronet became the beloved patriarch and patron of Newport until his death in 1906. He was involved in the Market Company, hotels, the brewery, the Literary Institute and innumerable social organisations along with his formidable wife, Annabelle. Already there were signs of decline as rents and income were hit by agricultural depression from 1870. He had no children and the estate was entailed to a series of elderly brothers who had no interest in the property and died at regular intervals culminating in the suicide of the fifth and last brother, Francis, in 1927.

Sir Francis Boughey was the last male, the eighth baronet, the seventh son of the third baronet and brother of the fifth, sixth and seventh. He was 79 and had succeeded in 1921. He had resided at the family estate at Derwen near Oswestry but then farmed at the Guild near Aqualate Hall.

The Times bluntly reported that he was discovered hanging from a hook in an outhouse at Aqualate Hall early on the Monday morning the 7 March. The actual building was the slaughter house. He had been well and active, following the hounds, and on the Sunday attended church and walked back to the Hall for lunch. He then went out and when he did not return for tea little was thought of it as he often stayed out calling. At eight a search began around the mere and over the dykes and at 3 am, all exhausted, the men came back for food and more men and lanthorns, when Gerald Clegg-Hill opened the outhouse door and found him hanging having been dead for hours.

The inquest at the Hall on the Tuesday brought in a verdict of temporary unsound mind Dr Elkington surmising that something in his brain had suddenly snapped and that if he had not hung himself he would have become hopelessly insane. The probable reason was his worry over the illness of his men and agent and the financial condition of the estate. The funeral was imposing there were over 70 workers from the estate, four clergymen and charabancs of mourners as well as friends and family. The cause of death was not mentioned just that he would be missed.

His generosity was said to be proverbial and certainly in his will he left his spaniels, his 12 bore shotgun, his motor car and £400 to his butler and, to his 'man' George Knapp, £50 to look after his pet terrier. Later, servants recounted how he was demanding and frightening banging the table for his breakfast of fresh eels from the mere and becoming irate with the butler if they were late. According to their story it was at breakfast he was found hanging on the landing and that the servants actually ate the breakfast first to delay informing anyone! Of such are legends made.

As there was no male heir the title went to a distant male relative and Aqualate was entailed to the four daughters, in turn, of the Rev George Boughey. Unfortunately the sisters could not agree on the future, leading to personal antagonisms and disintegration and dispersal of land and contents.

The inheritance became a cankerous obsession. However the part played by women in the demise of the estate began long before the sisters, with their aunt Annabelle Boughey wife of Sir Thomas Boughey.

Sir Thomas and Lady Annabelle

At her death in 1914 the obituary could not be more effusive after all she had been generous to the church, left a legacy to build a hospital and few in Newport had not benefited from her benevolence. After the funeral in Newport church hundreds lined the way to the town cemetery where a large monument stands to her memory. But in this simple sentence questions arise. Why Newport church, why Newport cemetery for the Lady of Aqualate when she was the patron of Forton church?

What was behind this bountiful façade, what was the relationship with her husband and her husband's family? Annabelle was the renowned rider, the "thorough sportswoman", while Thomas, though master of the hunt, was rarely at the front of the field. It was their failure to produce an heir in a family that could produce twelve or thirteen children each generation that caused all the later problems. In his will Sir Thomas had requested she be allowed to stay on at Aqualate Hall after his death, (1906), but she lingered on for sixteen months selling everything in the house causing friction with Sir George Boughey and his four daughters who were not able to enter the Hall until June 1908 by which time it was empty and "very small and queer".

Until 1906 there had been contact between Annabelle and the Rectory where the future Sir George had been rector for so long, she had visited the girls when they had measles, they had been to dinner and tea parties and walks around the gardens of Aqualate Hall but letters and diaries before that time hint that no one really liked her and that she ruled Sir Thomas with a rod of iron and was personally pretty ghastly.

Theodosia and Rev. Sir. George Boughey,
Ethel, Eva, Dorothy and Mary

The occupation of the Hall could be the issue for when Sir George after the funeral went to Aqualate to discuss business the interview with Annabelle was unpleasant. Contact ceased and Annabelle did not attend the wedding of her niece Dorothy in April 1907 which had to take place from the Rectory as Annabelle was in the Hall. When Annabelle finally left for Sundorne Castle near Shrewsbury the reaction of the Boughey family was "a good riddance".

Lady Annabelle was alone in a London Hotel when she died and was brought from there to the funeral at Newport church and here the quarrel becomes clearer. Few of the Bougheys were there still being in a huff from 1906 when Annabelle had written to Sir George Boughey saying she never wished to speak to them again or any other Boughey. She took the ill feeling to the length of not being buried with her husband but at Newport two miles away but only a couple of fields from his property. The monument says pointedly "Lady Boughey of Sundorne".

In 1932 a couple, Major and Mrs Pilkington, who had visited Sir Thomas and Annabelle when they were at the Hall recalled how they hated her, she was vulgar, arrogant, selfish and ill-natured as well as coarse and ugly. The seeds of decline had been sown.

The three daughters to whom the estate was now entailed do not appear to have learned from these family disputes for when Ethel Boughey (Morris) took over in 1927 she and Eva Boughey (Greene) quickly disagreed over the future of the estate with their sister Dorothy. The first daughter, Mrs Morris, took over an overdraft of £8,000, a hall still un-repaired from the fire of 1910 and dilapidated property and land. There had been little maintenance and no improvements. The land was in a shocking state, the mere, the brooks and drains all blocked and the place infested with rabbits, 700 being caught in one period of ten days. Added to this were death duties of £47,000 entailing the proposed sale of about 3,000 acres. Times were so bad that at the sale of 22 March 1929 only 500 of the 1,500 acres on sale were sold realising only £1,100. Plough Farm at Forton, 150 acres, fetched £2,000 but others were withdrawn, Coton Bank Farm at £4,500, the Red Lion, Sutton, at £990, Walton Grange Farm at £6,000, Bromstead and two cottages at £4,600, Manor Farm, Wilbrighton at £3,400 and four fields totalling 52 acres at £1,200. There were no bids for Outwood Banks Farm, 52 acres, though four cottages there went at £100, £70, £75 and £80.

Money was needed for repairs to farm buildings though older buildings were pulled down and materials re-used, and to renovate Aqualate Hall, estimated to cost £8,000 and not completed until 1934. As for income good tenants were hard to find, difficult ones harder to remove; sale of contents fetched little as did the sale of timber. In October 1929 the

Midland Coal Company who had much of the coal on the Audley estate, failed.

By 1956 Mrs Morris had about balanced the books but the trustees, as the estate was entailed, were forced to sell large portions of the estate again to pay debts and duties when Mrs Morris died.

Dorothy Boughey (Clegg-Hill) and her daughter Selina were farming Fern Hill on the estate and allegedly annoying their neighbours, trespassing by coursing or with greyhounds and beagles. Even the servants remember Selina exercising her beagles around the village to the annoyance of residents. Dorothy and Selina protested they were being persecuted while Ethel accused them of being dotty, mad or having some crazy sort of plan. Dorothy constantly insisted on alterations and repairs at Fernhill and when these were agreed left to live with Selina in London.

Ethel was 69 in 1945 and weak and bothered by business. She and Eva were anxious that their interest in the estate should be transferred to a younger branch of the family, Sir Richard Boughey, this would bring in a young, energetic male with money and unite the estate again with the name of Boughey. Selina, who had assumed the inheritance from her mother Dorothy, was made an offer for her interest but a dispute arose over the sale of the Aqualate diamonds which would have provided money for urgent repairs.

In March 1949 the large tapestry curtains made in the 1880`s for the Dining Room were finally thrown out as rags having been cut down and patched over 66 years to fit smaller windows. But poverty is relative and Ethel Morris led a full social life around the country houses, weddings, tennis, sherry, hunt balls following an accustomed pattern; she was involved in the Cottage Hospital, the Newport Agricultural Society, District Nursing, parish affairs and the WI; she was a regular follower of hounds on foot and bicycle and later by car and attended all the local race meetings, sitting on the committees; she was seen at Ascot and the Eton v Harrow cricket match where a Boughey was captain of Eton. She had several cars including a Daimler and always a chauffeur; there were five indoor servants, a woodman, carpenter and painter out on the yard, two keepers and two in the garden. The servants grew old with her.

Ethel and Eva angry with the delay, talks having begun in 1940, which saw their efforts at transferring the estate baulked, decided on a strategy of keeping niece Selina waiting as long as possible to succeed.

The next life tenant and sister was Mrs Eva Greene aged 80 when she came into possession and she was determined to spend the income, invest nothing and leave her younger sister a bare house, a run down estate and huge death duties.

There was little the trustees could do except carry out basic maintenance.

Mrs Greene achieved her aim by living reclusively until the age of 96.

Dorothy Clegg Hill was 95 when she inherited the burden of debt. To avoid duties she waived her right to the inheritance in favour of her daughter Selina and removed the entail and the trustees though it took nine years before the trustees were satisfied the liabilities had been paid and handed the estate as absolute owners to the Juhre family.

Whatever the rights or wrongs of the dispute the fact was the Juhre family took over an estate whose condition soon shattered any romantic illusions and nine years of struggle ensued before any of the great estate, the mere and the house were retained.

Longford, Chetwynd and Aqualate were always going to struggle in the twentieth century and it is a tribute to their loyalty and tenacity that they survived so long, but the Bougheys added personal animosity to the normal spectres of death, depression and taxation, which while ironically leading to the survival of the estate also led to its sad decline.

Writing in September 1947 having survived another war, Ethel Morris was upbeat "....the landed gentry are not finished nor England down and out. The old families on the land have done it before and are doing it again. Many have proved and are proving again that if you stick to the land the land will stick to you and if you do your duty by your land and your tenants you can carry on."

These were defiant words but the rural England once governed, planned and administered from country houses, the centres of large independent estates with the wealth and tradition to support private benevolence, had gone. Today the gentry and estates have been dispersed and with them the natural leadership, the social standards and their patronage and protection.

Mrs. Eva Green

Mrs. Selina Juhre

Town Versus Gown.

In February 1929 Walter Samuel Brooks, headmaster of Adams` Grammar School, William Harman and J.T.Lowe, assistant masters, were summoned before Newport Magistrates Court by Ernest James Wright, for assault on his son Frank Wright a pupil at the school.

Newport Grammar School, or later Adams` Grammar School, was founded in 1656 to provide free education for eighty local boys. By 1903 under the benign rule of the headmaster, Tom Collins, who had been there since January 1871, the school had only fifty pupils and had become a kind of gentleman`s club providing a few excellent scholars and eccentrics though most boys left before 14. Tom Collins was a large, affable man who because of his years and sheer size, and the few pupils, ruled by a benevolent code which did not require physical punishment or moral pressure. Collins made it a principle that the cane should not be used.

W.S. Brooks

Things were to change after the 1902 Education Act when Local Education Authorities were set up, in this case Shropshire County Council, to provide secondary education for all on the basis of fees and scholarships. Shropshire took the route of adopting existing Grammars Schools in the market towns such as Newport, and adapting them to the new system; Collins had to go, and he went, and a new headmaster was brought in with the task of taking boys unused to any training after the elementary stage and inducting them into a new system which would keep them at school until 16 and hopefully 18. It was similar to the Industrial Revolution of a century before when a rural country had to be moulded into a factory system requiring routines, regulations and discipline never experienced before.

112

The job went to J.W.Shuker who took a school that had lost much of its effectiveness and from behind a stern, formidable exterior ruled with a rod of iron. He terrorised boys into learning accepting no failures, no weakness, as measured against standards explicit or implicit. He rejuvenated and remoulded the school not without some opposition to his methods. Both he and his successor Brooks used the only code available, that of the public school and even today it is a code that the Grammar School aspires to. Brooks extended the public school ethos introducing Houses, substituting rugby for football and emphasising the prefect system a particular form of control which led directly to the 1929 court case. Brooks was a flogger, a descriptive word he deliberately used, and there was a climate at the school which accepted such as normal and more than that, as manly.

It is in the King's Bench Division that a precise account of the case is given: "At a school for boys there was a rule for prohibiting smoking by pupils during the school term whether on the school precincts or in public. During the term a pupil rather less than sixteen years old, after having left the school for the day and returned home, smoked a cigarette in the public street, and the next day the schoolmaster administered to him five strokes of the cane as a punishment for a breach of the rule. On the hearing of an information against the schoolmaster for an alleged assault on the boy the justices found that the rule in question was reasonable, that the father of the boy by sending him to the school authorised the schoolmaster to administer reasonable punishment to the boy for breach of a school rule, and that the punishment was reasonable; and they dismissed the information."

The report of the magistrates' hearing appears in the Newport Advertiser for 11 January 1929. The magistrates were the Hon Gerald Clegg-Hill (presiding), Messrs T Griffiths, R.J.Milbourne, E.G.M.Carmichael and J.M.Belcher. Mr Carmichael remarked that one of the defendants, Harman, had given private tuition to a member of his family, but no objection was made, regrettably, as Mr. Carmichael frequently interrupted in favour of the defendants.

The prosecution said that the circumstances were unfortunate and unusual and their case would be that the assault or chastisement administered by the defendant was unreasonable. Frank Wright had borne an exemplary character during his time at school, reports being endorsed "General conduct very good" and he had never received any punishment until the

113

flogging on the morning of 7 December 1928. It was the intention of Frank to leave school at the end of that term and join his father's business. On 6 December he had left school at 3.30, the normal closing time, and gone to his father's Picture House situated in the corner of the Market Hall with the entrance off Stafford Street. He assisted at the cinema. With James Williams he collected cases of film from the railway station and handed them to the operator at the cinema who gave then a cigarette each. The pair then walked down the High Street where they met a prefect named Bracey who acknowledged them and walked away.

The next thing they heard about this "enormous sin" was after prayers at school the next day when the defendant Brooks dismissed the junior school, the senior school remaining behind. Brooks then called Williams and Wright to come forward Wright being surprised as he did not know what it was for. The headmaster informed him that he had been reported for smoking in the street and asked if that was true? The boys replied that it was, upon which Brooks informed them that he was going to flog them. Upon that Wright dodged the headmaster who called upon the two assistant masters, the defendants Harman and Lowe, to catch hold of the boy. Wright then made a run for the library stairs, was stopped by two prefects, and a struggle ensued with the masters during which Frank Wright was badly knocked about. He was taken by force back to the headmaster and laid across a desk and his legs and shins put across the seat where he was held by Harman and Lowe and flogged by Brooks and, according to the prosecution, flogged in no gentle manner. There were marks on his body and on his shins. He was flogged again and told to apologise and being exhausted did so.

Brooks afterwards made a speech. Wright later went to his classroom and after asking if he could wash, ran home and complained to his parents. His coat and underclothes were torn and on his shin was a mark above one inch long. The weal marks on his body were inflamed and undoubtedly had been inflicted with great force. On discovering this, Mr Wright, in the opinion of the prosecution, quite rightly, went and complained to the headmaster of this brutal assault. He saw the defendant Brooks and between them a certain conversation took place which the prosecution alleged was the most material evidence they had of Brooks' attitude.

Mr Wright said that Brooks was pleased to see him but very excited and upset. He said Frank was a good boy, he liked him, he was a "sport" but he had broken a school rule and he had had no alternative but to flog him. Mr Wright then questioned this rule and asked to see it but Brooks argued it was a general rule and known. The prosecution argued here that even if the headmaster had jurisdiction over the boy after school hours, which they were not prepared seriously to contest, the punishment was not justified. Mr Wright maintained that the boy had not been warned, he was leaving in a few days and to hold him up this way before a large number of boys was uncalled for. Brooks denied he had thrashed him before a large number of boys.

The prosecution then described how Mr Wright told Brooks that he had received as Chairman of the Urban District Council, many complaints about the number of thrashings at the school. Here Mr Carmichael interrupted saying "Is this evidence?" Brooks replied he had thrashed only six boys that term as he could not do as he liked since he had a corporate body to deal with. The prosecution then alleged that Brooks apologised for the thrashing before Mr Wright left. It was after Mr Wright had checked the statement made by Brooks regarding the school beatings and found it was untrue and after Frank had been examined by a doctor that he decided to bring the case.

There was no doubt that a schoolmaster had the right of reasonable chastisement delegated from the parent but the punishment had to be in proportion to the crime, the offence must have been committed when the pupil was under the jurisdiction of the schoolmaster and the punishment should have be unobtrusive. Mr Carmichael again interceded quoting a case supposedly contradicting the prosecution who replied that in that case the master had been proved justified but the punishment proved excessive.

Frank Douglas Wright the pupil concerned gave evidence stating he had been a pupil for five years and became 16 on 11 December 1928, after the incident. Recalling the caning he said he refused to be beaten but did not say why. His coat had been torn in the struggle with the masters that had lasted several minutes before they laid him across a desk of the type where the back of the seat was level with the writing part; his shins were on the edge of the back and his body across the writing part. Lowe and Harman were holding him down, one his feet and the other his head. He had no idea how many times the Head beat him. The headmaster then thrashed Williams. Afterwards the headmaster told the masters to loose the witness who had been held down while Williams was thrashed and he was told to bend over again and without being held down was thrashed. He was then made to apologise to the school and the headmaster told the school he would give the same punishment to any other boy.

Frank Wright explained how he went home where his clothes and shirt collar were found to be torn and he had scars on his shins and weals all over his body. He contended that he had never been warned about smoking, had never seen a copy of the rules and did not know it was against the rules to smoke in the street and had only smoked in the street once before. He denied the evidence of a boy named Carpenter and others such as Bracey or Hoof under cross examination by the defence. His Form Master, Mr Ibbotson, had warned him that smoking in the street was indecent but not that it was against a school rule. He denied that he had deliberately tried to kick the masters and that he had flung himself bellowing on the ground. He said he was proud of the school. Referring to his return to school at midday to collect his belongings he denied he had used obscene language and threats to other pupil witnesses or boasted of the treatment he had given the masters. If they had said those things they were lying to support the headmaster. He admitted he did not know what perjury meant. To further questions from the prosecutor he agreed that his reports had been very good. Here the magistrate, Mr Carmichael, intervened again, considering such reports immaterial.

Giving evidence Mr Wright said he had never had a complaint about Frank in the five years he had been at the school. He described the injuries of the boy when he returned home, there being five swollen weals across his body and another on the back of the thigh down towards the knee which was very severe. The injuries were not bleeding but were very bruised and swollen. It looked to him as if the cane had been used with brute force. The skin on the shin was broken and the mark on the one leg over an inch long and on the other leg, one and a half inches long, and that mark still remained. Recounting the interview with the headmaster he said he thought the headmaster had flogged the boy in a most unreasonable manner and that it should have at least been in private where he was not exposed to ridicule in front of all the boys. Brooks replied that he had only administered punishment in front of a few boys from his own class. Going on to other alleged complaints about beatings by the headmaster, Brooks denied these but Wright had since made enquiries and found them to be true. He alleged that Brooks repeatedly said he was sorry, was nervous and excited and seemed frightened of him so that he had to assure him that he had not come to do him any harm. At this point there was laughter in court. He was not angry in fact he felt sorry for Brooks seeing it as a sign of weakness for a headmaster to have to resort to corporal punishment. If Frank had deserved punishment he would not have objected to it in the headmasters study but he did object to him being thrashed in front of the boys and to the way he had been thrashed.

The defence began by disputing the injuries and the damage to the boy, arguing any that had arisen had done so by the action of Frank Wright in refusing to take his punishment. The injuries were his own fault. The statements made by the Grammar School witnesses to their solicitors Hodge, Harries and Elliott, still exist and make interesting comparisons to their evidence in court. The headmaster Walter Samuel Brooks stated that on the evening of 6 December 1928 a prefect, Frederick Bracey, came to his house and reported Wright and Williams for smoking in the town High Street. He decided to take stern action because the act was deliberately defiant to a school rule, both boys were senior members of the school, they were both under the legal age for smoking and the street behaviour of both boys had been causing anxiety to the school. This behaviour including not wearing a school cap, he himself had seen Wright not wearing a cap three times that term. He had gathered from other staff that Wright was increasingly antagonistic to the headmaster's attitude to public behaviour and that as Wright was leaving, prefects had begun to turn a blind eye to his behaviour. It was because of his influence on Williams, an able boy, a popular athlete and much younger, that he felt action was needed. The school behaviour of Wright had been such as to give Brooks the impression that his influence amongst the boys was subversive. He had been reported about eighteen months ago by a prefect for disrupting the preparation room and he himself had noticed the same thing on entering the room. Preparation was a period after school in which boys, including day boys, returned to school to do what is now called homework. Wright had not attended prep for a fortnight and had not offered an excuse.

Brooks then described the caning, including the fact that there were about 75 boys and 7 staff present out of 240, hardly a "few". He gave Wright 3 strokes over the desk and then another one while bending down. Wright then collapsed on the floor and after getting up received a fifth and final stroke with a "normal sized cane." He then described the interview with Mr Wright alleging that Mr Wright stated that only his public position prevented him dealing with Brooks the way Brooks had dealt with his son and that his brother-in-law had once assaulted a schoolmaster. Wright was also alleged to have said that Newport was ringing with Brooks' brutality. The Head explained that physical punishment was preferable to detention. Mr Wright, in further conversation, said that the Head had banned day boys from taking girls to his Picture House. Brooks appeared to believe he had answered all Mr Wright's points and urged that the matter be forgotten and Frank come back to school as he was a good athlete and should not end his days under a cloud. Mr Wright was then supposed to have told Brooks that he was willing for Frank to return but he doubted whether his mother would allow it!

Brooks said he had only ever received one complaint about punishment and rarely used corporal punishment and then only after careful consideration that it was warranted. Brooks also suggested at this point that any injury to Frank Wright had occurred when he fell down a staircase at school.

In his evidence in court Brooks said he was not frightened by Mr. Wright in fact he was glad to see him. He rarely threatened or caned boys but considered it far worse to be expelled than be caned. He was not sorry for the thrashing but did prefer boys to take their punishment voluntarily. Frank was a good lad, he was not going to say he had been a bad boy all along, but the punishment was reasonable and Frank should have taken it in a manly spirit. Brooks could not say whether his blows usually marked a boys flesh he had never examined them or considered the effect his blows would have, though he had a "shrewd idea" they would leave a mark. He had punished him before his fellows in order to make it "impressive" and to support the prefects. To say it was a deterrent Brooks thought a very unfair question. Here we have Mr Carmichael asking why the prefects did not cane, administering what he called a "monitors whopping". Mr Brooks demurred at this saying it was not usual in schools of the Grammar School type. He did not know if flogging had been carried out at Newport before he came.

William Harman in his statement supported the Head stressing that he and Lowe were in considerable danger from Wright struggling and kicking. He also intimated that Frank Wright could not have been too hurt as he saw him that evening with a girl down Cock Yard. He repeated this remark in his evidence alleging Frank was having a "jolly time" and got the expected cheap laugh.

Leonard Ibbotson, Frank Wright's Form Master, confirmed he had warned him about smoking, in front of the whole class and had told him no smoking was a school rule.

Several boys gave evidence George Carpenter in a statement and Frederick Bracey and F.M.Newrick in court. Bracey confirmed the evidence of the headmaster and said the punishment "was administered absolutely in the ordinary way" though he had never seen anyone held down before. Newrick had been with Bracey in the street when they saw Frank Wright smoking. Newrick said he had never smoked in his life which was remarkable as his father was the local newsagent and tobacconist a business which Newrick took over and ran for years. George Carpenter said three minutes after the caning he met Frank Wright running through the Annex and bragging that he had kicked Mr Harman and got a good one in on Lowe. He repeated the boast at Prep that same evening. He also recalled an occasion when Wright had said if he was caught smoking in the street he would refuse to be punished. Frank Wright returned to the school twice that day to collect clothes and is alleged to have made threats to other boys saying his brothers would get them. In front of several boys he told Bracey "you are a f...... c... and you ought to be b...... well ducked twice." There is no doubt that Frank Wright was far from a spotless, pleasant character.

Jim Williams the other boy punished also made a statement but this did not confirm in every respect the statements made by the masters for example in the number of strokes administered. He too said he had never been warned about smoking. Jim went on to be an excellent sportsman in cricket and football and a schoolteacher. He wrote poetry and accounts of his wartime experiences and remained a prolific smoker to the end.

At the end of the case the chairman remarked that they were clear that the headmaster was quite within his rights to administer corporal punishment. The boy knew perfectly well the rule of the school and there was evidence to show he was warned twice before by prefects and in November by a master. He deliberately broke the rule and in addition led a younger boy astray. Frank Wright had deliberately taken up a defiant attitude which was nothing less than insubordination and it was this that had caused the Head to seek the help of other masters. The damage done to the boy was of his own making. The case was dismissed. The defence asked for costs and were allowed £5.05.00 with a parting shot from the chairman that "The bench consider the case ought never to have been brought."

For the school it was the end, the event was rarely mentioned again. It was not the end for Mr Wright, a garage and cinema proprietor, who got his hands dirty and was a popular and generous man to the town and a member of most organisations. He had become Chairman of the Urban District Council, topping the poll in 1929, and by virtue of this position, a Justice of the Peace. His standing in the town would push him to appeal. It was his standing which in some ways led to the dismissal of the case for the establishment saw him as a man above his station, someone who should be taken down a peg or two. Certainly in the school there was a sense of getting back at Frank before he finally left and the whole thing imploded when he refused to acquiesce in the code. The shock, horror and indignity which this caused led the establishment to dig in, close ranks and deny the shame of the whole incident.

On 14 January 1929 Mr Wright made an application in writing to the justices in which he stated their decision was wrong in law and asked them to state the case on which they had made their decision, this case would then be considered by the Divisional Court of the King's Bench Division presided over by the Lord Chief Justice. By a certificate dated 22 January 1929 the magistrates refused, saying they believed the application was frivolous and therefore they would accordingly not state a case. Mr Wright replied by obtaining in the High Court an order calling on the justices and the schoolmasters to prove in law that they had the authority to punish the boy when he was out of school and under the control of his father. On 16 March 1929 the magistrates complied and made an answer in reply to the order saying the prosecution during the court hearing had never questioned the right of the school to inflict such punishment only basing their case on the footing that the punishment was unreasonable, excessive and unreasonably administered. As we have seen the judges dismissed the application by Mr Wright considering the magistrates had correctly applied the law, there was a school rule, the punishment was reasonable, no law had been broken so there were no grounds for charges of assault and no need for the magistrates to explain their actions. The decision entered the educational law books and made legal history.

The case made the local, national and international newspapers and opinion was divided. On 18 January Mr Wright himself wrote to the

Newport Advertiser disassociating himself from the scurrilous campaign against the parties concerned. There were no details. Another letter from Mr S.E.Cottam MA Oxford was against the decision asserting that no headmaster had any authority to treat pupils in any such way. "My sympathy is entirely with the boy and his parents who are strangers to me." He continued "No headmaster of a day school is warranted in asserting his authority over his pupils when they are off the premises. It is the parents who are then in authority. Smoking is not an offence at all; and to inflict corporal punishment for it in any case is wrong, and, as a young man of sixteen, monstrous. This is an evil from which we can only be delivered by a reign of reason."

An octogenarian Old Boy named Levi Chilton from Four Ashes, Wolverhampton, wrote saying he thought it was a disgraceful action by the three masters and that previous heads had been perfect gentlemen and that the masters had let the school down. "I feel sorry that the three masters have disgraced the character of the school. When I was at the school the three masters - Dr Saxton, Mr Heywood and Mr Crowther - were perfect gentlemen. They knew how to put it on when necessary, but never were brutes. A lecture to a young man of sixteen, with an apology ought to have been sufficient for such a trifle. I have held the school in the highest respect since I joined it and was sorry to hear of its disgrace."

Another writer, "Fair Play" of Newport, asked did the prefects smoke, who reported them and were they caned? "Many people, including myself, find it somewhat difficult to understand why certain prefects of Newport Grammar School who have habitually smoked in the main street, were not flogged with Williams and Wright. When school reassembles next week if the headmaster is consistent and has any sense of fairness, he cannot do less than see to it that these prefects receive the flogging due to them according to his code." The writer named the prefects; the Advertiser declined to print the names.

Mr Alfred Fellows of Lincolns Inn wrote "...is it not the ordinary pedagogue`s horror at the thought of his charges smoking cigarettes rather old-fashioned in these days? In nine cases out of ten he smokes himself and the veto survives from the days when those who wished to smoke were sent to the kitchen after the servants had gone to bed." Masters smoked, Leonard Ibbotson, the form master involved, often walking out of the smoke filled staffroom. Masters had been known to send pupils out for cigarettes, "Billy Bloggs", alias Mr. Hoggins the

121

history master, would confidentially whisper to a boy to "nip down and get a packet of Gold Flake from Midgleys". A public schoolboy driving through Newport reported that the case had led to graffiti on the walls and thought it deplorable, while a public school housemaster supported the caning. One writer pointed out that flogging had been abandoned in the army and navy why not in schools?

The Daily Mail also carried letters but the cruellest response came from the magazine "John Bull" once controlled by Horatio Bottomley a convicted swindler who, in 1920, had put up an "independent" MP in the Newport Constituency ironically supported by Mr Wright. The magazine agreed with the decision and suggested that it would have been in the best interest of Mr Wright not to raise such an outcry over the caning. If mature men in the academic profession found it (caning) necessary to secure discipline then we, said John Bull, may rest assured they are acting for the best. Mr Wright should have done more to make a man of Frankie by letting him take his punishment like a Shropshire lad. This theme of "manliness" occurs throughout the affair.

"Le Soir" in France on 8 January condemned the flogging as a tradition in the United Kingdom and therefore sacred. They compared the case with one in Leeds where a woman had to pay £25 damages and £10 costs or go to gaol for having thrown boiling water over a dog while the Newport magistrates had dismissed a case for thrashing a boy. "Corporal punishment in English schools is an abuse against which protests have been made in vain, because it is a tradition and in that country to interfere with a tradition is a sacrilegious act."

Mr Ernest Wright died in 1933 after a long illness but Walter Brooks went on teaching, exonerated and compensated, until he retired in 1944. He carried on caning. In 1939 or 1940 boys were put to pulling up the long grass on the Shuker Field so that Sports Day could go ahead. A prize was offered to the boy who picked the most grass but because they all clubbed together in the task no one received the prize and they were all caned. Another pupil recalls that the then caretaker had two sons at the school one of whom could be quite a tearaway and who had the temerity to cheek Brookes in front of Mr Harman's class. Brookes who always carried a cane thrashed the boy across the face with it and desisted only when physically restrained by Mr Harman. Very young pupils in 1945 understood that you did not linger near the Headmaster's study door. By 1944 Brookes was deep into religion, counselling the 6th Form on religious facts and life and proclaiming religion "... can be caught but it cannot be taught." After his retirement he became a minister in the Church of England in the south of France.

The official history of Adams' Grammar says "Sam" Brooks came with a reputation for caning and the injustice of his punishments rankled for years. As well as boys, young members of staff and parents were scared of him. Scholarship boys and their parents, who had little influence, were treated roughly and the boys usually placed in the B stream from where they had little hope of higher academic achievement. The Wright family were in this category. But there again Brooks ignored everybody including the County Council education authority. The authors conclude that today Mr Wright would win his case not, we hope, because corporal punishment is illegal, but because such a barbaric exhibition to satisfy the ego of one man, would not be tolerated.

Many years later one Old Boy who was at the school at that time, being interviewed for something completely different, remarked that Brooks was a sadist.

Frank Wright was rescued from Dunkirk.

Frank Wright

The Newport Shootings.

It has been said that depression, anxiety and suicides decreased between 1939 and 1945 under the greater tension of warfare. Individual problems were submerged in the community of purpose and involvement in the common danger. This did not apply to Newport for in March 1943 occurred a tragedy which wiped out a whole family and shocked the town; yet this was a period of optimism when the end of hostilities seemed realistic; El Alamein had seen Rommel defeated in the Western desert in October 1942 and then in January 1943 twenty one German divisions surrendered at Stalingrad and Hitler's defeat was inevitable. At such a euphoric time a local disaster was the more shocking.

What was the tragedy? The bodies of a man, his wife, his son and his wife's aging mother were found in two bedrooms of their double fronted house on the outskirts of Newport. The dead were Ernest Edward Leek aged 47, his wife Flora Ann Leek aged 44, his son Alfred Ernest Leek aged 6 and his mother-in-law Mrs Susan Ann Taylor aged 81. The dead man was the manager at Messrs Baker's boot and shoe store in the High Street one of the best known figures in the business life of the town. In the six years he had been in Newport he had won a coveted reputation for high business integrity. His unruffled demeanour and happy smile, which was his most engaging feature, had won the respect of all who knew him and for someone who had not engaged in public life, he was extremely well known.

He hailed from Newcastle-under-Lyme where he was the son of a boot and shoe merchant Mr Ernest Edward Leek. After leaving Newcastle High School he assisted his father in the business until the Great War intervened after which he entered the service of Messrs Lloyd, Evans and Co. the Stafford boot manufacturing concern. He was a foreman until the works closed down when he joined Bakers. Prior to his appointment at Newport he was an assistant manager at a Wolverhampton branch. Bakers had acquired the Newport business of R.H.Turner six years earlier and Leek had been manager there from 12 August 1938. Originally a thatched cottage the premises were rebuilt in 1845 but had housed shoemakers since 1797 and still sell shoes today (2010). During the 1914-18 war Leek joined the 5th Battalion of the North Staffs Regiment and reached the rank of Sergeant receiving a bayonet wound in his arm in the fight for the Hohenzollern Redoubt. Like many others he rarely spoke of the war but to those who knew him his experiences had left an indelible impression, yet he was one of the first to volunteer for the Home Guard quickly becoming a sergeant and soon afterwards he was commissioned. He was the oldest officer in A Company of the 11th Battalion, Home Guard.

He married Mrs Leek, who came from Stone in Staffordshire, in 1925 and soon after they were joined by her mother, Mrs Taylor, widow of Alfred Taylor from Stone, a storekeeper who had died in 1915. The little boy was a pupil at the Infants' school in Avenue Road.

Baker's young assistant arrived at the shop from her home in Sutton on the Tuesday morning just after 8 am to find that Mr Leek was not there. After waiting some time she went off to have a word with another assistant who worked part time in the shop and together they went to Mr Leek's house but their knock on the door brought no response. They could see that the blackout had not been removed from any of the windows. They reported it to the police station and PC Davies and PC Welch went to investigate.

The two constables being unable to get into the house broke down the back door and the first thing they encountered was a quantity of plaster and a bullet on the floor. The ground floor revealed nothing but on going upstairs they found in one bedroom the bodies of the two women both with mortal gunshot wounds to the chest. Mrs Taylor was in bed and Mrs Leek was stretched out on the floor near the bed, both in night attire. In another bedroom they found the body of the boy, in bed, with gunshot wounds and across the bed was the body of Leek in pyjamas with gunshot wounds to the chest. Beside him was a Browning automatic rifle of the kind used by the Home Guard, the magazine of which held twenty bullets. It looked as if Leek had reversed the rifle and touched off the trigger with a stick. At that time the cause of the tragedy was a complete mystery.

The Wellington District Coroner opened the inquest on the bodies at the house on the Wednesday afternoon only formal identification being given by PC Henry James Taylor of the Staffordshire Constabulary, brother of Mrs Leek. The inquest was then adjourned until the following Wednesday at the Town Hall.

On the Tuesday evening at the weekly parade of No 2 Platoon at the Home Guard headquarters, Major E.S.Christmas the Company Commander who was the local baker, attended along with his deputy Lieut. H Davies and after roll call explained what had happened to their platoon leader and after two minutes silence the parade was dismissed and the men quietly dispersed.

The inquest was resumed on Wednesday 10 March at Newport Town Hall before the Wellington coroner Mr J.V.Lander and a special jury. The foreman of the jury was Mr Archie Brooks. Representing the police were Superintendent F Withington and PS Harrison, for the Home Guard, Major Christmas the officer commanding, Capt. F.S.Whitwell, battalion adjutant and Acting Captain Harold Davies. Also present were Mr Arthur Leek of Shelton, Stoke on Trent and Mr Victor Leek of London, the dead man's brothers, and also PC Taylor of Stoke, the brother of Mrs Leek.

The first witness was Dr. H.M.Shenkin, the local doctor, who was called to the house about noon on 2 March and found four people dead with gunshot wounds nearly all in the chest. Only Leek's wound, he said, could have been self-inflicted. Mrs Leek was on the floor and Mrs Taylor was dead in the same room, both had an arm fractured by a bullet. Mr Leek and the boy were in another room, the former lying at the foot of the bed and the child in a natural sleeping position, covered by the bedclothes, apparently having died immediately after being shot. The two women appeared to have lived for a few minutes. All the deaths appeared to have taken place 10-12 hours earlier that is approximately midnight. Leek was lying on his left side with the muzzle of the gun pointing at, and held firmly against, his chest. The stock of the gun was propped against the bedclothes.

PC Davies said that about 8.30 am on Tuesday 2 March he was informed by the shop assistant that Leek had not been to the shop that morning and that going to his house she could get no reply to her knocking. She believed something was wrong. At 10.45 he and PC Welch went to the house where he found the blackout still up with the exception of the sitting room window at the rear of the house. The doors were all locked on the inside so they had to force an entry through the back door. In the kitchen on the table were the remains of a supper, a collar and tie, a wallet and a bunch of keys. The door leading to the staircase was closed and on opening it at the foot of the stairs inside the front door he found a quantity of plaster on the floor and a bullet-hole in the ceiling above. The front room door was shut and the room in good order.

On going upstairs the constable found a spent rifle bullet on the fifth stair and another one on the top of the stairs. In the bedroom on the left was the body of the boy lying in bed wearing his nightclothes which were saturated in blood while his eyes and mouth were wide open. He had a large wound in his chest. Along the bottom of the bed was the body of Mr Leek in his pyjamas lying on his left side. The muzzle of a Browning automatic rifle was against his chest and the butt of it near the pillow. Near the trigger was a piece of stick. He had a bullet wound in his chest and an exit hole in his back.

In the adjoining room he found the body of Mrs Leek on the floor beside the bed with her head resting on the bottom stay of a bedside table. Her nightclothes were saturated in blood and she had extensive wounds in the chest and right arm. On the bed was the body of Mrs Taylor in night attire lying on her right side in a normal sleeping position. She too had extensive wounds and the bedclothes had bullet holes, scorch marks and were soaked in blood. There were seven empty cartridge cases and two more bullets and marks on the door and wall cupboard where the bullets had struck.

In the room occupied by Mr Leek and the boy the constable found three empty cartridge cases and an indentation in the pillow which suggested that Leek had been in bed. On the bed near Leek was one of his slippers the other being found near the door of Mrs Leek`s bedroom. There were night lights burning in both rooms. Here he found five live rounds of .300 ammunition and a colt or .320 automatic pistol and in the downstairs front room a box containing mixed ammunition including eighteen rounds of .300.

The witness said that he failed to find any letter in the house or at the shop and enquiries had found no debts but a substantial bank balance. In answer to questions the constable said that the trigger had been pressed using the stick there was no other way. There were still seven rounds in the gun. No one had been up the stairs after the family went to bed because the dust and plaster on the stairs was undisturbed. Replying to the foreman of the jury, PC Davies said that Leek must have taken his own life and the lives of the other persons.

Major Christmas was asked to describe Leek's behaviour before the shootings and to explain his possession of such powerful weapons and large amounts of ammunition. Leek had attended the Officers parade the night before and appeared perfectly normal. He had had conversations with him before when he appeared worried but he did not know what about. For several weeks he had seemed overstrained but he had not given a cause. On one occasion he did say that a certain incident connected with Home Guard administration was in line with everything that had happened to him recently, that he had been doing things "backhandedly" such as writing letters to the wrong people and that anything that could go wrong had gone wrong. However after that last parade he had said he was much better. As for the Browning automatics, Leek, as platoon commander was entitled to hold two and had borrowed a third from another platoon for instructional purposes. He was not entitled to hold ammunition though in the early days of the Home Guard officers had held ammunition. By 1943 all ammunition should be in the Company storeroom and had to be returned there after issue. It was Leek's job to do this. However without a full-time storekeeper who never left the store it was impossible to check all ammunition. Again it was not certain that it was Home Guard ammunition, Leek had many friends in the military world and in other quarters and anyone wanting ammunition could get it. Leek was particularly interested in rifles but as for the automatic pistol he did not know to whom it belonged but it was not someone in the Home Guard. As far as his private life Leek had never confided in him.

After the parade at about 10pm Leek and a Mr Parry went to the Vine Vaults and had a beer and discussed Home Guard affairs around the fire. The licensee, Thomas Wilde, recalled serving them and said Leek was perfectly sober and rational and he had never seen him any different. He knew him well but nothing about his private affairs except he was extremely fond of his little boy.

Leek's brother-in-law said to all appearances the family were happy, there were no worries and Leek was temperate and hardworking. A neighbour echoed this adding that Mrs Taylor lived quite happily with them and they were devoted to their boy. The women had been ill and at times appeared worried but as she was friendly rather than intimate with them she did not know why. The family had few visitors. On the night in question she heard Leek come home a little later than usual and a bang in the night which she attributed to a vehicle. She heard nothing more and as far as she knew there was no trouble there during the night.

Crucial evidence came from Richard Butler a director of Baker's. He said they took stock every six months and on 14 February 1943 they found a deficiency at the Newport branch of £230 whether in stock or cash it was difficult to say. Enquiries had been made and Leek asked to explain but he could not. No accusations had been made and there would have been another stocktaking to confirm the loss. This could have been sufficient to disturb him. There had been a deficiency in November 1941 of £90 which Leek had partly repaid others had been normal and they were satisfied with his work. As long as a man did his work they never enquired as to his private life.

Summing up, the coroner said the trouble at his work would account for Leek being not quite normal. The jury having retired for about half an hour said they were of the opinion that the women and child met their deaths by gunshot wounds inflicted by Leek who met his death in the same manner by self-inflicted shots. They said Leek did this while the balance of his mind was disturbed.

The funerals took place on the Saturday, Mr and Mrs Leek and the boy being buried in the same grave at Newport cemetery in the morning and Mrs Taylor at Stone in the afternoon. There were military honours with the coffin draped in the Union Jack with the Home Guard Company providing the escort and the bearers. The escort met the cortege outside the Town Hall and led the mournful procession through the High Street, Upper Bar, Avenue Road and Audley Avenue to the cemetery. It was led by a drummer, and a bugler sounded the Last Post and Reveille at the graveside. There was no firing party.

And so under the shadow of a terrible war, private grief and tragedy went on.

Hey-Ho Come to the Fair.

In May 1939 after 800 years the May Fair folded its stalls, hitched up its rides and vans and left the High Street where it had stood since the Middle Ages, never to return. In fact medieval Newport had been designed and built for the simple purpose of staging annual fairs and weekly markets and when the fairs and the markets disappeared so did the soul of the town.

Newport was a planned town long before Telford highjacked the concept and being a simple plan was the more effective and probably longer lasting. Two entrances at the top and bottom led to a street with buildings either side with long burgage plots which serviced the frontage businesses. The street widened in the middle to create an island site for a provision market and church and capable of holding large numbers of livestock. The whole was carefully placed on the county boundary where roads met, now the A41, and others led to Shrewsbury and Stafford. Here also was a safe crossing of the meres. Politically it was no-man's land tucked into a corner where four parishes met. Add plenty of water and a thriving fishing industry in the meres and you have the recipe for a successful settlement.

There were at least eight such towns in Shropshire all strung along the county boundary with Royal Charters that gave the burgesses freedom to set up markets and fairs, for goods and pleasure, and protected their trade, and whose tolls supported the Lords of the Manor. They were business investments of the new Norman owners to exploit the resources of their estates. The catchment area, particularly for markets, was about 5-6 miles - Donnington, Hinstock and Gnosall - but for fairs with more specialist goods such as cloth, wool and metals, dealers were prepared to travel long distances within and outside of Shropshire despite the condition of the roads.

In 1319-20 wool was being carried from Newport to London by the Kings carthorses from Adderley, and in 1356 goods coming in included leather, skins and coal. In 1670 buyers came from Wellington, Cheswardine and Staffordshire while in 1700 store cattle were being bought at Newport Fair, buyers travelling long distances. On 17 July 1318 Sir John de Chetwynd had a market and fair at Chetwynd in an attempt to acquire some of the "profits to be derived from the droves of cattle which came that way out of Wales to relieve the famine which was then desolating a great part of England; and both would be glad to set up a rival to Newport, which was fast becoming a thriving town." It appears that Chetwynd had a three day fair on All Souls Day, 2 November, and also a market but was suffering from the proximity of Newport.

Writing in the 1880's T.W.Picken recalled that "Numbers of Welsh cattle used to be driven through the town in those days en route for London and many droves of ponies. We used to watch them carefully and any special pretty or fine animal we used to try to be the first to cry out 'bags that'."

There were problems as in 1748 during a cattle plague when on 14 May Shropshire Quarter Sessions ordered "that no ox, bull, cow, calf, steer or heifer be bought or sold in either of the said fairs" that is the fair in Newport on the 17 May and Wem on 25 May.

Fairs were not only for agricultural products, from 1718 we find the partners in the Coalbrookdale ironworks travelling to fairs in North Wales, Cheshire and Staffordshire selling pots and pans, taking orders and collecting coinage, often in short supply, to pay their workers. As late as the 1870's a man bought his fourth wife at a local fair! Picken believed "In olden times these Fairs were of great service not only for business and pleasure but they acted as link in promoting intercourse between the villages and the town and were looked forward to with interest by the country people."

In 1763 there were said to be five fairs in Newport, 28 May - the one that continued till 1939, 27 July, 10 September, 10 December and Palm Sunday. "Owens New Book of Fairs 1820" has Newport Fairs on the first Tuesday in February, 28 May, 27 July for horned cattle, horses and sheep, 25 September for cattle, sheep and hogs and the 10 December for sheep, hogs and fat cattle. The Horse Fair was traditionally held in the High Street in front of Temperton and Temperton, formerly the Old Bell, and the parish register of 28 November 1663 records the first horse market in Newport.

From 1750 onwards the character of fairs began to change, nationally the large ones began to specialise - Northampton for horses, Worcester for hops, Ipswich for butter and cheese. Around London many fairs became assembly points for trade with the city while in hundreds of small towns in England and Wales, weekly or fortnightly markets took over much of the trade previously done at fairs. Some of these markets kept the dates of the traditional fairs by having specialist markets such as horses and cattle on the old fair dates.

In 1837 the Newport Fortnightly Cattle Market Committee was set up to regulate the markets but also to take over the work of the traditional fairs. By 1851 the chartered fairs had merged into the fortnightly cattle market held every alternate Tuesday except for the fair of 28 May which continued. They were well attended but other local markets, such as Shrewsbury, had also transformed themselves and organisers looked anxiously to see what effect this would have on the buyers coming to Newport.

On 16 August 1856 Henry Fisher a local solicitor and secretary to the Cattle Committee gave notice of a horse fair by permission of the Duke of Sutherland the Lord of the Manor, to be held annually on those fortnightly cattle market days which coincided with the old fair days in February and September in addition to the Horse Fair in May.

The fairs had been swallowed by the markets but very quickly the street markets also were to disappear forever. By the 1850's the fear and depression of the "Hungry Forties" was being replaced by confidence and prosperity. Townsfolk were fed up with the obnoxious condition of the open livestock markets, the smell of the dead in the churchyard, the lack of clean water and sewage, the disorder and violence in the streets and the lack of effective local government. On 29 March 1856 the Newport Advertiser took up the cause. "Many of the inhabitants complain bitterly of the intolerable nuisance in allowing cattle to stand on the causeways and that bulls should be allowed to be brought into the town. When the causeways are flagged, it is quite clear that some alteration must take place, and it is to be hoped that before long a suitable Smithfield will be established outside the town."

A contemporary humorist saw Newport as a place "Where Fair is foul and Foul is Fair". In 1854 a new Marsh Trust completely repaved the streets with granite setts and relocated the water mains, getting rid of the stagnant water cisterns in the middle of the road. £2,200 was raised, a third by public subscription. The Market Act of 1858 set up the Market Company removing at a stroke the cattle and provision markets to a purpose built market hall and livestock market in Stafford Street costing £13,000, all raised locally. They have never been allowed to re-appear. Public pride, visionary men, the courage of local investment regenerated a town in ten years. The fair and the market went separate ways and all there was now in the High Street was the annual May Fair and a smaller one at Christmas, the "Gawby Market". The medieval fair had become a "Pleasure Fair" and many would have liked to abolish that.

1855 and 1856 saw the last two fairs with the traditional mix of trade and pleasure. The 1855 May Fair held on a Monday saw a scanty supply of livestock as if the sellers were anticipating the coming banishment from the streets. As this was a traditional horse fair there was a good supply but prices were high and few horses changed hands. The numerous menageries and side shows were absent owing, it was thought, to the Fair falling on the Whit Monday when stallholders were in more profitable locations and the "many excursion trains to different parts" caused a meagre attendance. The railway was to play an important part in the future of the Newport Fair. Meanwhile Mr Barnado Eagle with his clairvoyant lady was in residence in the assembly room of the Royal Victoria Hotel obviously not having foreseen the poor crowds!

The Annual May Fair of 1856 passed off quietly with the usual rows arising from drinking sprees - this was the decade of the Newport Irish. The Horse Fair had a large supply of horses and many changed hands but there were few cattle and pigs and consequently prices were high. The pleasure side was described as the "Children's Fair" and included gingerbread and fancy toys and amusements in the shape of swings, shows and rocking horses. The newspaper seemed rather disappointed that little work was required from the police who kept a vigilant lookout for pickpockets who generally frequented the event.

The new cattle market was opened on 14 December 1858, until then the cattle remained on the street and as the Market Hall was not opened until November 1859 so did the provision market. At the 1857 May Fair the cattle, horses and pigs were actually sold at a new market down on the Marsh, while the pleasure fair had the usual children's entertainments but Wombwells menagerie, which came to the May Fair for over seventy years, did not appear and the other exhibitions were below average. The Advertiser, rather smugly, felt "This species of amusement appears to be on the decline and altogether the fair was not as large as previous years." Very dull, was the opinion on the 1858 May Fair with a peep show, a learned pony and two "swarthy fellows" under canvas engaged in "pitch in". There were stalls for toys, sweets and gingerbread while a few had carriages with a flying hare at which customers could shoot for a halfpenny. Most loose change went to the coffers of the public houses.

133

The whole parade of the Fair, said the Advertiser, was going down, with education making an inroad into it; "...decay is written upon it, its glory has departed". It had declined socially the time having gone when high born dames and men renowned in business made an effort to be there and money changed hands freely. The town, said the editor, would be better off without it, trade would not suffer, and an immense amount of immorality and vice would be avoided.

Unfortunately for the newspaper, 1859, possibly because it was the first pure pleasure fair, attracted the greatest number of showmen for over thirty years, within living memory. For over three days caravan after caravan pulled in to Newport all looking as if they had been on the road for ages. There was a vast array of shows, Automatons, Peeping Toms, Billy Buttons, Bell Horses, cheap jacks, cake and nutsellers and riflemen. There was every sign that plenty of fun would be provided and it was hoped that drunkenness would be absent and that the "gay lads and lasses" would enjoy themselves while not being offensive to others. There was however the "usual profligacies and drunkenness on the street to the annoyance of the peaceable inhabitants". The Advertiser found some consolation in the thought that with so many showmen the competition would ruin them.

Numbers were considerably less than former years in May 1860 owing to it being Whit Monday with the railway companies putting on numerous excursion trains which had taken the crowds away. There were few attractions, a stray show or two and a rifle gallery but, most conspicuously, a boxing booth with over the entrance portraits of the recent contestants for the Heavyweight Championship, Tom Sayers who was an 11 stone Englishman and the Benica Boy, an American, three stone heavier. This was a bare knuckle fight for high stakes which went on for over 37 rounds before being broken up by the police. The next year such fighting was banned and the gambling aristocracy lost interest but it shows how the fairs kept up with current events and attracted the public. Sayers retired with over £3,000, an absolute fortune. By now all the markets were in the purpose built livestock and provision markets under the 1858 Market Act and only the amusements were left in the street.

Over the next three years visitors and stalls varied in numbers - but not the "roughs" - until by 1863 it was said the fair was but a shadow of its former self. However the Advertiser of May 1864 referred to "..this great annual pleasure fair" with large numbers of shows and exhibitions if not spectators. The great attraction for the editor was Wombwell's menagerie and in an ecstatic article he described how Wombwells had first come to Newport seventy years before and for over twenty years their show had been the only means of educating the young people of Newport in the natural world and the beasts of the forest, and even though railways had broadened their horizons and the great zoological gardens of London and the cities were in reach, such collection of animals, he felt, were of use and were admired by the country folk. Mrs Wombwell, who was still coming to Newport after fifty two years should be supported, for the risks and costs of caring for, feeding and transporting such wild beasts, were enormous. However a letter in the same edition bewailed the orgies of the fair which had become the focus of drinking that was ruining the working country men and women who wheeled homeward to be frequently maimed or killed on the road. Such drunken crowds, such noisy shows endangered the lives of ordinary people. Who would, the letter pleaded, come to the rescue of Newport?

Wombwell's Menagerie on the road.

Meanwhile in early May 1868 one of Wombwell's lions died aged 45 at a show in Oswestry, to general grief.

Showmen needed publicity and were expert at stunts such as the one in May 1868. One exhibition was a "living skeleton" whose bones were scarcely covered in skin. This show also involved a snake on the stage outside and while climbing a ladder to unwind the snake the skeleton man fired a pistol which was just charged with powder but caused a nasty mess of his hair and face, and fright and confusion to spectators. However later in the evening the living skeleton far from being dead was perceived on the stage again! There were other freaks, the largest horse, the smallest lady, a cow with legs on its back and a fat boy. There were also two or three theatres, a waxworks exhibiting the latest - Todmorden - murderer and by 1870, whirly-gigs and merry-go-rounds. There were camels that had walked to the fair and showed it. There appeared to be more drunkenness in 1868 but temperance was on the march and the drunks were advised they would be better off at the Temperance Festival which was taking place at that time in Lilleshall. By next morning not a vestige of the fair could be found in the High Street.

In the 1880's the newspaper tended to ignore the fair, reports were short and comments derogatory even though the street was packed with amusements and customers. The fair, it said, was a mockery, a delusion and a snare, showing signs of rapid decay with the latest steam organs shrieking and groaning their repetitive tunes. People were not as gullible with the advent of cheap and compulsory education and the depressed state of industry and jobs, and even the cartloads of labourers and colliers no longer came and spent their savings. In the newspaper's opinion fairs were a thing of the past acting as they did as an excuse to drink. In 1885, 1887, 1888 and 1890 there was no report at all.

By 1886 T.P.Marshall had joined the Advertiser, a reporter with aspirations as a wit - he labelled himself as "Office Boy" - raconteur and writer who did not use a word where two sentences would do. Excusing the flowery language and the humorous social commentary he gives a fine atmospheric insight into the event, the drums and gongs, rattles and cymbals, the brass players, the German band (string), and the steam organs that grew louder as the night got darker. The standings along the curbstones between the Kings Arms and Addisons, had Emma stalls, and "Brummagen jewellery" with keyless watches and chains for 2d. Near the Vaults was a new set of hobby horses dressed as "foxhunters" which ran on wheels and swayed from side to side, the venture of a new showman, P Collings (Collins). Then there were the Waltzing Cars and Caddick's photographic studios. Near the Butter Cross was an "excelsior exhibition" with performing birds and a hare that played the tambourine. By the Advertiser office was a favourite show of the "Mermaid" and on the other side, by the Raven and Bell, a "Zulu" dressed in dirty skins who spouted gibberish and then walked on fire. However the showmen were not beyond sneaking out of town at night without paying for the pasturing of their horses! Then came the moralising from a nonconformist, temperance, newspaper; the fair was an orgy it said, squalid and vulgar, that would die out as education improved and people went on cheap excursions to the seaside, and yet, it confessed - the crowds did seem to be enjoying themselves!

Our effusive office boy was back again in June 1889 wandering through the noise in the glare of the naptha lamps describing the usual amusements, including a stick and ring stall and an egg and bottle shooting saloon, the gaily painted vans and the gaudy carriages, and, to him, the crowning glory of the fair, Manden's Royal Moving Waxworks with its golden facade, its organ and exhibits including Napoleon, Jackson the Manchester murderer, Buffalo Bill and Royalty. At the Butter Cross was a huge van where models such as waterfalls, birds and lace making were worked by steam power. One caravan set on fire but was that another gimmick?

There were great changes in the 1890's; local government was reorganised and the new Rural and Urban District Councils began to enforce licenses and tolls; steam engines which had powered the rides now produced electricity and people flocked in to see the lights as later they went to the illuminations in Blackpool; more importantly there arrived Pat Collins, a showman extraordinaire from a dynasty of showmen that included the Fossett, Davies and Harris families who still operate today.

The local newspaper ignored the fair in the 1890's except for two contrasting reviews in 1893 and 1895. The report of 1893, though admitting the fair was on an "elaborate scale", is completely negative with mean, cheap and spiteful remarks on the un-cleanliness and coarseness of the showmen, the nauseous, loud and sickening music, the inconvenience to the traffic and doubts whether anyone in Newport benefited from the event. On the other hand on 1 June 1895 there is a detailed account and a long interview with Pat Collins the greatest showmen of his age, a remarkable social document that gives the flavour and atmosphere of the old time fairs. For the first time the Advertiser appears to acknowledge the scale of the fair and its importance in the life of the community, though it still had niggles. Now the fair had become an "institution" and its showmen and proprietors were gentlemen of "many years standing".

The May Fair this year was huge, completely swamping the character of the town not only with the huge array of attractions but with the enormous crowds that poured in during the evening. The main attractions were Mr Gottheimer with his roundabouts and Pat Collins with the Venetian Gondolas outside the Vine Vaults, the prime site. These were linked up with electricity from powerful traction engines which provided the bright lights and overwhelming music. There were all the conventional stalls, coco-nuts, confectionary, boxing booths and ice-cream, which was a totally new experience for the country folk. On the morning of Wednesday 29 June when the fair had cleaned up and left Newport the reporter found Mr Collins in his private carriage parked under the Market Hall at the top of Stafford Street. Aged 36, born in Chester, he had started with his father and then gone on his own in 1881 with just £5 with a set of swings and two doll stalls at Wavertree in Lancashire. Like most showmen he was prone to exaggeration. He added a set of roundabouts and reckoned to take between £20 and £50 a site. By 1895 he was based at Walsall and the family had four tours around the country for six months beginning in February, employing 150 men. They also had a menagerie and pavilion at New Brighton which they called the "World's Fair 2".

He maintained he had been coming to Newport since 1875 but he is first mentioned in 1886 with his hobby horses as Mr "Colling". Certainly it was his endeavours which restored Newport Fair from the 1880's and by 1910 it had become an important outpost on the No.1 circuit even if transport was lengthy and the one day "gaff" endangered profits. Newport Fair lasted so long because it was on the circuit routes from Birkenhead to Birmingham and Llangollen to Longton. He thought the 1895 fair was the largest he had ever seen in the town and as he and the reporter chatted in the Barley Mow he claimed he had over £1,000 worth of stuff in the street and over £5,000 worth of goods in total in Newport. He claimed also to have developed the Venetian Gondolas but it was more likely he bought them second hand; what was true is that he had a new Burrell traction engine, the no. 1777 "Emperor", plus six portable engines which had been supplying electricity for five years. Like many of his critics he would have liked the Newport Fair not to be in the High

Street because he could have taken his time in arriving and erecting and would have avoided the statutory restriction of one day, which he mostly avoided anyway. As for his private caravan, described as cosy and convenient by the reporter, it had cost £350, a colossal sum in today's (2010) money and was a reflection of his success.

The 'Emperor' Church Square Newport 1900

The showmen were having to face the growing powers of Local Government, first the District Boards of 1875 and then their successors the Urban and Rural District Councils of 1894. One example will suffice, the meetings of Newport Urban Council in May and June 1897. After three years in existence the Council was feeling its feet and asking questions. Councillor Sir Thomas Boughey, no less, wanted to know who collected the fair tolls and why the shooting galleries were in the street when everyone knew they were dangerous? Others were suspicious that the Fair was continuing beyond its allotted day. The surveyor was instructed to find the answers. The next month, after the Fair Day, the Council Committee ascertained that the tolls for May Day were £4.12.00 (£4.60); they objected to the extra days, (many showmen were still there at midnight on the 29th), for which of course they could not collect tolls as they were strictly illegal, while Sir Thomas said no one benefited from the fair except the publicans and if anything the fair took people out of the town. They should abolish the fair as it was a nuisance to every respectable tradesman and person. Put it down Audley Road, he said. The truth was, as pointed out by Mr Gottheimer, the showman, it was uncertain as to whether the Council could summons or prosecute the showmen. These disputes about the collection of tolls and the legality of the street fairs lasted until the 1930's when the Fair ended.

Until 1914 the Establishment of Newport continued to snipe at the fair. The authorities had a reasonable argument for in 1905-06 the Marsh Trust, the body whose income was devoted to the maintenance of the streets, had re-laid High Street and St Marys Street with granite setts at a cost of £1,705, and the Council, quite naturally, were reluctant to let the fair men continue to hammer in their spikes to hold up the various attractions. In December 1905 they restricted the Christmas Fair to one stall and that pitched at the side of the Market Hall in Stafford Street, they also started to mark out the pitches with whitewash as another method of control. The Urban District Council took further steps to remove the "ancient fairs" petitioning the Home Office to this end and approaching the Market Company to enquire if the fairs could be moved to the livestock market. This led to a petition in May 1906 to the UDC signed by 263 residents, or was it 252, including eighteen publicans out of twenty-two, asking for the fairs to be retained in the streets. The UDC stuck to its guns pointing out to the publicans, that the Vine Vaults, where the main attractions were always sited, had not signed the petition! Of course this did not stop the UDC collecting the Fair tolls, £3.19.00 in 1899, £5.06.03 in 1903, £5.09.09 in 1904 and £18.10s in 1908. By May 1911 Pat Collins was paying them £10 per day, really a bribe, to stay open for three days instead of the statutory one, as well as donating generously to charity.

Meanwhile the Advertiser had changed tactics after the death in 1904 of Charles Horne the last of the nonconformist, Congregational, teetotal founders of the newspaper. Its main complaint, up to that time, about the fair, real or imagined, had been its drunkenness and debauchery, now it emphasised the damage and disruption to the town - traffic continued to use the street, there were no diversions - and its legality. The issue became "The Newport Fair Question" in 1906 and emerged in editorials, not as opposition to the Fair "as such", but because of the damage to the streets and the archaic medieval right of "piccage", literally the right to hammer your stall into the ground. The tolls did not even pay for the damage done to the street. The fairs should be done away with, removed elsewhere as they brought no benefit to the town and served no good purpose. The other tactic was to ignore the event, to deride it and make it the object of humorous articles by its resident columnist, George Aspin, to simply make fun of the fair. We find the attractions labelled paraphernalia; "a miserably poor affair"; shorn of "its pristine glory" a fair which has "discarded its utility". More coverage was given to the death, and the inquest, of a worker erecting the switchback in the Square in May 1906 than the fair itself.

At this time another prophet arose to damn the Fair, Mr Shuker, headmaster of Adams Grammar School, who believed, as did others afterwards, that the school had the curious right to universal control of its pupils. In 1911 he complained of the noise and the overstay and in May 1913 went further saying the fair was a disgrace and could not understand why the authorities allowed it. He banned boys visiting the fair unless with their parents. There were letters of protest. As late as June 1937 another Grammar School headmaster was expressing concern over the possible ill effects on the health of the district from the fair.

Despite the adverse comments reports show, and the records of Pat Collins prove, that by 1914 the Newport Pleasure Fair was an enormous success, a massive event in the social calendar, looked forward to with great expectations by country and town alike. Technology had vastly improved transport - the fair now travelling by rail, one truck catching fire at Gnosall in 1913 - and the size and variety of the attractions, while the publicity skills and entrepreneurship of Pat Collins was too much for rural politicians. In 1899 the newspaper admitted the "large scale" of the fair; in 1901 it was "largely attended"; in 1903 it could not deny the fair was "the largest that had been for some years"; by 1906 "the merriment ran high", there was no horseplay or drunkenness or anything to regret about the behaviour of the crowd. In 1907 the residential caravans stretched from the Market Hall down Stafford Street to Water Lane, and there was no room to pass down the High Street while the crowds were there from 6 pm to midnight.

For the children in these poverty stricken Edwardian years the fair was a long felt need which head-teachers ignored at their peril. In 1900 and 1914 the Junior School gave a half day for the fair; a half holiday in 1903 was for the fair and the circus which was held in the field behind the school. The fairs usually came with a circus or a menagerie. The Catholic School had a holiday for the fair in 1902, and in 1906 "The school was closed on the occasion of the annual May Fair in the town.

Only 49 children put in an appearance on the next morning." There were 69 on roll.

From 1910 the fair was at its peak and for the first time the camera proves it. The Advertiser was anticipating large crowds and more attractions than previous years particularly the "Wonderland" show with its organ by which the fair was extended for three days and allowed the sacred concerts. Through this attraction Pat Collins gave £28 to the Hospital Sunday Committee in 1910 and £3 from the roundabouts and the whole of Tuesday's takings in 1911 when the fair was a record breaker.

The reports of May 1913 and 1914 give us a final taste of an Edwardian Pleasure Fair before the Great War destroyed that life forever. It opened on the Saturday and continued until the Wednesday night described as Pat Collin's World Fair with a scenic railway and a real waterfall. The "Palace of Wonders" presented by Mrs Collins, with its superbly carved entrance, had been the talk of the town for weeks and the first part of the performance was a display of cinematograph films followed in part two by the "new" Lafayette, Mr James Lee, with his illusions and tricks, baffling reason and logic. Solid objects came from nowhere, shadows materialised, as did rabbits and birds on the wing. Comely ladies and curious gents appeared and disappeared including Zaro the "suspended lady". There was a large variety of side shows and minor attractions. The reaction of the reporter was complimentary praising the high standard and urging that that the fair be patronised. 1914 had the scenic railway, Manders Bros African Jungle, freak shows in one of which a fat lady was the central figure. There was Dirty Dick (if you hit the right target he fell into a bath), shooting galleries, a photographic studio and the "other characteristics of a modern fair." A "modern" fair, praise indeed, to lead us into a "modern" war.

Surprisingly the fairs continued to come to Newport during the war and were advertised in the old enemy the Advertiser. By 1916 the editor was lamenting that the fair used to be "one of the great events of the year" and that year was combined with the war effort, a fundraising "Russian Flag Day", but, not unexpectedly, by 1918 the fair had diminished almost to vanishing point.

Despite the world wide flu epidemic which killed more people than the War, 1919 opened with optimism which for a few years seemed justified.

Pat Collins' Fair Newport High Street - early 1900's

By 1921 the boom had ended and then came the events which today define the inter-war years, economic collapse, depression, unemployment, poverty, strikes and political extremism. Add to this poor weather - at least where the fairs were concerned - and the misery was complete. More and more Newport looked to its May Fair to lift the gloom and Pat Collins did his best.

The May Fair of 1919 enjoyed hot weather and if some of the former attractions were not there and the crowds were not so large or as boisterous as before the war, nevertheless there was enough to make it enjoyable. The hobby horses had been updated, there were bowling booths, throwing galleries - darts now as well as rifles - while along the north side of the Market Square there were stalls for ice cream, gingerbread, toys for the children and baubles for wives and sweethearts. The dust-stained clothes of the crowd showed how far they had travelled, from the villages and the industrial towns, while the yards of the pubs now stored not only bicycles and waggonnettes but motor cycles and motor cars. For some reason the fair was a fortnight earlier in 1920 occupying the area from the Advertiser office, then at 23 High Street, right down to the Grammar School, with the living vans lined up against the Town Hall wall in Stafford Street. The Square had the most popular rides, the motors and hobby horses and a stand where birds picked out cards to tell your fortune. In front of the Advertiser were football nets while in front of the church was a boxing booth and a "Jazz" attraction. Given the motor traffic the Urban District Council now had some road closures in place.

It is possible to know more about the fairs from 1920 because we have the recollections of people who witnessed the event. One young man from Edgmond recalled riding his bicycle to meet his girl friend at the fair, passing a revival meeting at the church gate then the boxing booth then going into the "Jazz Hall" which was a kind of swing boat. After ice creams they struggled onto the motors in the Square, five girls and one male packed like herrings. Not surprisingly "It was a glorious ride and the organ played delicious music. My female companions, too, were very pretty, and I had one on each side of me!" The roundabouts followed and lastly a freak show, an elephant faced man, but, although only a model, "Jane fainted, so I took her home."

One young lady from Bishop's Offley was an assistant in the Newport confectioners Elkes Bros in 1920, which was situated behind the Butter

Cross in the middle of the fun. Near the shop window was the helter-skelter a tower down which you slid on a mat in fact many people called the ride "the mat". The gondolas were in the Square and the boxing booth below the church. The surprise for her was how quickly the fair came and went arriving on the Tuesday and by Sunday morning there was not a trace left. At 11.50 on the Saturday night she recalls the National Anthem being played on the fairground organ with everyone joining in then standing in silence as the church clock struck twelve, then the goodnights, the packing away of the stalls and the dismantling of the amusements, the swish of the water cart on the streets and the brushing of the pavements and the return to the peace and quiet of a Sunday morning.

The fair was described as the great event of the season in 1921 filling the High Street from Lower Bar to Upper Bar a magnificent sight when illuminated at night. The crowds were huge, estimated at thousands, coming from great distances, despite the pouring rain on the Saturday night. The Helter-skelter Lighthouse -"the mat"- again stood at the Butter Cross and from the top there were splendid views of the surrounding countryside. There were the popular rides in the Square, the numerous stalls and the freaks which this year included a racehorse and a lamb both with five legs. Pat Collins intimated that he would give a benefit performance on the Sunday IF the council would allow him to open on the Monday, they did not, leading to numerous letters of protest at the decision, asking why, hinting at council chicanery and bewailing the loss to the charities as well as the traders. The council replied it had already given permission for three days, well beyond the statutory requirement, and would have given a fourth if a proper request had been made. Pat Collins was again weaving his web, trying his tricks.

Newport Fair could not escape the world depression which set in from 1922. Unemployment was rife in the area and it was obvious that the large crowds had less to spend so much so that on the Saturday night, May 1922, Pat Collins did not increase the prices as was customary. The weather was glorious and the attractions and the crowds as large as before. In front of the Grammar School was a lion show including the largest African lion ever imported, pure forest bred. In the Square was the scenic railway worked by electricity with a splendid organ and a waterfall, with the cars shaped as dragons. There were galloping horses on the roundabouts, swing boats, arcades, slot machines and dozens of stalls. A visitor was struck by the lion show and the bravery of the coloured lion tamer who entered his den and that of the three lionesses.

145

The lion tamer was actually "Maccomo" known to his friends as Albert Williams while most of the lions had been reared as cubs by Pat Collins' alsation dogs! The visitor was fascinated by the two dwarfs and their baby and a grim exhibition of the life of Landru the French Bluebeard, including his execution, though he was unsure as to whether the latter was "amusing". For the next few years the fair brought some magic to dispel the misery.

Unemployment and low wages continued to affect the fair until 1927 but the attractions rolled up from the spectacular to the macabre. Moving such large rides caused huge logistical problems but as heavy vehicles - many being bought second hand from the army after the war - and electrical technology improved, such features could visit rural towns like Newport. The Helter-skelter Lighthouse stood outside Elkes', the Gondola roundabouts in the Square, the steam yachts (giant swingboats), the Whales (a roundabout), Over the Falls (a continuous conveyor belt which gave a bumpy ride from the top of the falls to the bottom), the Razzle Dazzle (a roundabout that tilted and dipped as it rotated) which smashed the window of Masons' butchers shop when being dismantled in 1925, all appeared in turn well into the Thirties.

As for the macabre they included Tiny Tim the Lancashire midget, 35 years old and weighing only 24lb, wearing a top hat and standing next to "Colosso" a nineteen year old Scottish boy weighing 44 stone; there was also "Lolo" a mysterious girl's head which appeared without a body, and then a "Victim of Opium". There were snake charmers and a black African Chief Nyambi and his Acunakim warriors performing their rites and customs. In May 1927 Mr Henderson the landlord of the nearby Plume of Feathers sat in the lion's cage and drank a glass of beer and smoked a cigarette. For some years the newspaper failed to report even such outrageous stunts.

Another dimension was added to the Fair in 1929 with a beauty parlour with performances by the Cabaret Girls portraying living statues of works of famous artists - shades of the Windmill theatre. Another lady, "She", was chained, locked, tortured and stretched 30 inches on a rack, the proprietors maintaining she was the talk of every town she visited. An African chief, this time Wambo, bent red hot bars with his feet and hands and licked them with his tongue.

Meanwhile the Urban District Council and the Market Company were still disputing the control of the streets and the rights to the market and Fair tolls. In 1921 the Market Company leased the bottom part of the Market Hall to Wright's garage and the indoor stalls were put up in the Square opposite the Market Hall. The Council claimed the tolls and the rents, marked out the stalls and stands for the Fair and cleaned up the mess left by the Friday markets and the fairs. Anyway the Council wanted the Square for the parking of buses and cars. The Company took the initiative calling meetings with the Council seeking the advice of Counsel and called a public meeting to air the dispute. The Council threatened to summons any stallholder in the outdoor market the Company retaliating by saying they would pay the fine of any stallholder convicted. At the subsequent court case the magistrate levied nominal fines for obstruction. By now the High Street was being designated a trunk road under the control of the County Council and this brought in the County Council surveyor who asked under what powers had the UDC given permission and the Ministry of Transport, who said nobody had the right to permit the fairs, though in fact the Minister turned a blind eye until the fairs ended naturally with the outbreak of war. Because of this dispute it does mean that there are no outdoor markets in Newport as there are in such towns as Market Drayton and Bridgnorth.

Dragon and Peacock ride, in front of Vine Vaults 1933

147

Pat Collins continued to play the differences between the two authorities to his own advantage. Except for bad weather there were organ recitals on the Sunday of the Fair now attended by the Chairman of the Council with collections for the Hospitals, in fact one councillor was threatened that if they did not sanction the extra day for the fair it "..would be the death knell of the Council". The importance of this fund raising and an indication of the poverty of the town is illustrated by the fact that in 1933 the Hospital Committee only had enough funds to distribute £40 and the Fair had raised a quarter of that. Collins also cleverly continued to pay £10 to the UDC for the right to use the streets at Christmas though there is no evidence that he had more than one stall. Albert Brotherton (1908-2003) remembered the coconut shy and the Wall of Death but never a fair at Christmas.

The "Death Globe" was a feature of 1933, a motor cyclist riding around the walls in an enclosure with a lion roaming around underneath; there was also for the first time a Ghost Train. Also there were motor cars which the occupants steered themselves; were these the first dodgems?

Joe Gardiner, an old showman, brought the miniature racehorse and the largest pig in the world to the Fair in May 1935. The horse was only 23 inches high, weighed 5lbs and was five years old while the pig was as large as an ox over eight feet long, seven feet round and weighed over a ton. He was impressively insured for £5,000 and his body destined for the British Museum. However the real sensation of the fair was a fire which started in the Dodgems on the Church Square destroyed the canvas roof and two other tents these tents coincidently containing the little horse and the gross pig. Billy the pig used his massive frame to destroy his pen and was gently shepherded into the Plume of Feathers "to the consternation of the customers" though he is said to have behaved impeccably. A large crowd witnessed the valiant efforts of the fairground staff and all was normal quite quickly. A stirring tale except that next week's paper carried a small paragraph saying the fire was extinguished by three members of Newport Fire Brigade, W.H.Gregory, J Sandbrook and W Porter with a hose from a street hydrant within a minute of the alarm. A "sensation" just a little too neat and obvious?

The May Fair slipped from the headlines appearing as a notice of coming events or as an advertisement. In 1936 the public was advised that Pat Collins would be bringing the scenic railway, the Jungle Stampede - "60 miles an hour and 60 thrills a minute" - and the Auto Scooters de Luxe -

"Dodgems". Harold Pyott took out his own advertisement advising people he was the smallest man in the world, just 23" high, weighing 24 lb and 49 years old. Despite his measurements he was apparently called up for the army three times during the Great War! Known professionally as Tiny Tim he had been in Newport in 1923 and now issued a challenge of £100 to any man over twenty to run, jump, swim or wrestle who would come down to his weight. Born in Stockport he was buried there in 1937 aged fifty.

The famous Waltzer came in 1937 and 1938. A large advertisement in 1938 promised the world's best attractions, fun, frolics and thrills and the greatest riding devices ever seen. "Follow the crowds to Collins' Great May Fair" was the slogan; "Super Dodgems - the last word in cars on the track"; "The new motor cycling speedway - first time here"; "The Waltzer - will whirl you into merriment"; "The Jungle Stampede - 60 thrills a minute" and "The Airways - twenty flying stunt planes." However, the particular attraction was the Moon Rocket imported from America. On 29 May 1938 came another "Grand Sacred Organ Recital" on the scenic organ with proceeds going to Newport Cottage Hospital and the Hospital Committee. The concert commenced at 8.15 pm and programmes were 2d. Collins exhorted Newport "to roll up in your thousands". The Cottage Hospital received £10 from the proceeds. We know nothing about the 1939 fair except it must have been the last on the High Street and that for some reason the "Wall of Death" with roller skating and amazing acrobatics with high speed motor cycles, was held on the yard of the Shakespeare Inn.

In 1940 and 1941 the May Fair was held in the Town Meadow in Wellington Road behind the present police station, closing at dusk. The rallying cries were "Banish those blackout blues" and "there'll always be an England and a Pat Collins Fair" but it was not to be, Pat Collins died in 1943 and the fair went with him. "The street fair was rendered inadvisable for obvious reasons" was the official view while Albert Brotherton thought "The May Fair eventually went down Wellington Road because all the lights had to be out by a certain time on the High Street". Ray Elkes recalls that "When the A41 was declared a trunk road one of the most notable changes was the disappearance of Newport May Fair from the streets. The Trunk Road Act put an end to it all". It was as simple as that.

The end of the May Fair, as with the end of the livestock market in 2003, severed the link with Newport's rural past, it removed the reason for its existence.

What about the Christmas Fair? This was one of the original Charter or Statute Fairs but became inextricably connected with the "Gawby Market" both being held on the same day and considered as one in folk memory. My father used to call me a "gawby market" when I stood around doing nothing, a term of reprimand and abuse in country areas. Literally that's what it was a specified day and place after Christmas when country labourers would come into town and stand around to be hired for the next year having just been paid their twelve months wages - less deductions - for the previous year's hiring. They would line up to be viewed by the farmers and a deal struck for the next year sealed with a shilling (5p). The new job would start on 1 January till the next Christmas and would include ale, food and lodging. Workers would turn up with their tools or a symbol of their trade, a shepherd with a crook or a tuft of wool, a cowman with a wisp of straw, a dairymaid with a milking stool and a housemaid with a mop which is why some hiring fairs were known as "mop fairs". The Gawby was a jobs market where farm servants and labourers were matched with employers.

The fair dated from the time when agricultural workers, the bulk of the population, had to offer themselves for hire by law and there were attempts to control wages. This was because of the Black Death in 1348-9 when two thirds of the population died, workers were scarce and villages deserted. Disease was not limited to humans there were plagues affecting cattle and sheep caused by a dramatic climate change, a decline into an ice-age, into floods and famine. Land values, prices and wages went haywire and the Statute of Labourers, limited wages to existing rates of pay and insisted such pay deals should be done in public. Like today it is doubtful if such controls worked nevertheless they remained on the statute book for centuries, virtually gone by 1814 during the industrial revolution and gradually falling into disuse as the century went on, through farm mechanisation, newspaper advertising and more mobility with the railways and finally, with the Agricultural Wages Act of 1924, becoming a medieval curiosity.

Hiring fairs could be lively events as the workers had a years' wages to spend, a years' fun to catch up on, and showmen were not slow in taking advantage. So, like the May Fair, the Hiring Fair, the Servants Fair, the

Mop Fair, call it what you will, became another pleasure fair, attracting showmen, pedlars, tricksters and the disapproval of many.

In Newport the hiring fair was traditionally held on the first Saturday after Christmas and if this was not possible by special arrangements hence the "Special Pleasure Fairs". Like the May Fair by the mid 1800's it had become mainly for pleasure though as reports still talked of country folk flocking in it is difficult to know whether this was for pleasure or trade. One of the first descriptions is by a child of the 1840's who recalled, if the weather was fine, they would be sent out into the main road into Newport to see the gawbies coming in, women with large shawls and men wearing red plush waistcoats some with black or other coloured stripes. The tanned skins of calves in those days were made by country men into waistcoats with added sleeves to make jackets. The men all appeared elderly, worn out from working the land in all weathers.

The fair of December 1857 still appeared to have a hiring purpose as it was described for servants leaving their places. The day had to be changed as the original one fell on the day after Christmas nevertheless many "Johnnies and Mollies" attended to join in the various freaks and fancies put up for their entertainment. Numerous people visited the town to make purchases before entering their new situations such as boots and clothes to last them the year. A "Johnny" was a term for a simpleton and a "Mollie" was a foolish women. The fair of December 1858 appeared a more sober affair than usual with the country folk spending the surplus from their yearly wage judiciously rather than letting the showmen and publicans empty their pockets. The next year the fair was altered from the 27 to Monday the 31 and there were a considerable number of servants of both sexes.

By 1864 the purpose of the fair was changing with little business done and most intent on pleasure so much so that four years later the fair was described as a mockery with no amusements to speak of, no great number of servants and awful weather; December 1869 was no better and the weather worse. The fair "for the enjoyment of servants" in December 1870 saw "most unpropitious" weather yet there was a good attendance of country people to enjoy the merry-go-round, the one or two shooting galleries and the gingerbread stalls in fact it was the hobbyhorses and the attached organ that was the feature of these Christmas fairs until the 1880's, without them the event might have died out earlier. By 1884 the Gawby Market was a poor affair with Davies' steam hobby horses and one or two stands; the "Newport Advertiser" mused that perhaps the gawbies were being changed into wiser men and women and children though it would be unfortunate to lose something which did good to the town even for once a year. Yet the authorities, in this case the Marsh Trust, saw nothing wrong with the pleasure fairs for when they were petitioned by tradesmen and other inhabitants in December 1868 and December 1869 for permission to hold a fair the trustees thought it "desirable to hold a pleasure fair on that date."

This was not the view of some eminent Novaportans, two letters appearing in January 1881 deploring the Gawby Market with its scenes of vice and wickedness and filthy and disgusting language and requesting religious leaders to take a stand against it. The other letter berated the "Town Council" for not taking action against "a monstrous profanation of every good principle of virtue implanted in our nature". The fair was a deformity "of the darkest period of the darkest age" and the showmen, who erected their hideous abominations in the street, were "peripatetic mountebanks". The fair was a "blot".

That there was a drunken element taking over the event was well illustrated in the most famous riot in Newport's history in January 1882 when a group of Irishmen who had been convicted of drunkenness at the Christmas Fair fought the police all through town. This led eventually in January 1888 to a prosecution for obstruction of the highway against the showmen led by a letter of complaint from Mr Liddle, the solicitor and influential townsman, the Mr Liddle, who as a Marsh Trustee, had thought the fair "desirable" in 1868 and 1869. Such gentlemen opposed the fair others equally agreed with it and since no one could decide who had the right to permit the fair, collect the tolls from the fair or even prosecute the fair - the Market Company, The Marsh Trust or the local council - the magistrates fined the showmen a nominal 6d (2.5p) and costs, and things went on as before.

In fact the December 1887 fair had been well attended by showmen and customers and was reported as well conducted with a great deal of fun and little drunkenness or riot; the steam organ ground out "Two lovely black eyes" until past midnight clashing with the bells ringing in the New Year. 1888 was poor but 1889 saw lots of fairs in the district which called into Newport with their swing boats and hobby horses and numerous stalls. A local curiosity was a five-horned ram from Knighton Hall exhibited to raise money for Adbaston Church. Any drunkenness was excused by the bad weather causing visitors to seek warmth in the pubs but generally the proceedings were remarkably free from disturbance. The "old custom is fast dwindling away" was the comment on the 1896 Gawby and many young people who had worked hard in the countryside all year found little to amuse themselves. Again in 1898 the village folk were there but not the attractions and the Christmas Fair of 1901 was "not much of a fair" with just the regulars, Carlomen and his steam racers, some shooting galleries, egg saloons, swing boats, a weight tester and other stalls. 1902 opened on Boxing Day again with Carlomen and his friends. In 1904 the opposition of the Urban District Council and the newly repaired streets limited the fair to one stall at the top of Stafford Street while in December 1906 no attractions turned up at all, not even a gingerbread man. The same happened in 1908 leading to an editorial the following December in which the Gawby was declared as soon obsolete. Once called the Gawby Market then upgraded to the "Servants Pleasure Fair" it was going because those once characterised as "gawby" were disappearing as country children became as well schooled as the towns. The whole event was declining nationally as those who once came in to be hired and to spend their lump sums on clothes and enjoyment were no longer paid that way - it was now a weekly wage - few lived in, or had had the traditional jobs. There were fewer agricultural workers and those could well obtain employment from newspaper advertisements. By 1911 there was a meagre attendance and few servants turned up. Carlomen was still there in 1912 but the next year, December 1913, the fair was confined to three stalls, the old character had gone and the gales blew bitterly all day. That was the last one reported. Six hundred years of custom went and was wiped from memory by the war - except the £10 Pat Collins paid at Christmas to keep his options open.

Where Has What Was Ours All Gone?

In 1989 Newport lost its Cottage Hospital. In 1948 it had lost its ambulance and its Nursing Home, Roddam House, where many Novaportans had been born. The magistrates courts went in 1953, the railway in 1964. In 1974 our Councillors departed for Telford, by 2000 the livestock market, the historical reason for Newport, and Serck Audco its main industry and claim to fame, had also gone. Perhaps worst of all in 2009 Woolworths disappeared from the High Street! As they say, to lose one could be regarded as a misfortune to lose several could look like carelessness and requires some explanation.

What is interesting is how people reacted to these losses, some losses arousing shock, horror and outrage with eminent people jumping on the bandwagon and as quickly jumping off when it stopped rolling, yet other losses aroused little response though just as crucial to the life of the town. The hospital was a very emotive issue while the demise of Serck Audco, a disaster for the economy of Newport, caused hardly a flutter.

Before we look at the death of the hospital let us consider how we took care of our health one hundred years ago. At rock bottom was the Poor Law embodied in the workhouse which was loathed and feared and did not have an infirmary until 1908. Another way was "self help" through the Friendly Societies, organisations of working men then defined as shopkeepers, tradesmen and craft workers, which provided benefits in sickness, unemployment and death.

It was the Friendly Societies that were behind Hospital Sunday, an organisation found in most small towns. Hospital Sunday raised money to pay for tickets for people to travel to hospitals as well as giving donations to these hospitals. The first Hospital Sunday in Newport was held on Sunday 28 March 1875 when a procession of 600 - 700 people and a church service raised £36 which was given to the Shrewsbury and Staffordshire infirmaries and the Eye Hospital, Shrewsbury. In 1878 there were complaints of the lack of support from the Roman Catholic and nonconformist members, the latter apparently objecting to the filling of public houses on Sundays and the fact that three quarters of the tickets went to the Irish. As well as the procession and service, boxes were placed around the town and in the churches. In 1883 when the parish church was being restored they began to hold the annual service in the Market Hall, with over 2,000 people there in 1893. The 1897 Diamond Jubilee of Queen Victoria saw the biggest effort with £87.18.00 collected and in 1898 alone 86 people travelled to hospital through the fund.

Mr H.R. Lunn who was the Honorary Secretary and a printer by trade, produced and distributed posters around the town in 1903 calling a meeting for Saturday, 21 March at 7.30 in the Marsh Trustees` Room in the Town Hall, to make arrangements for that year's service and procession; the meeting it said was "...open to all Persons who are inclined to co-operate in the work."

In 1903 the Newport Advertiser carried a full report of that year's Hospital Sunday. The weather, it said, militated against the usual large gathering but the service in the covered general market was well attended. The committee was:-

> "Mr W Sambrook, chairman; Mr J Bate, vice-chairman; Rev W Budgen; Messrs T Williams, R Morris, R Blythe, J Heatley, J Wickstead, S.L.Roberts, L Bradbury, J.J.Jackson, F Talbot, H.R.Lunn, hon sec., (printer); A Nelmes, (coachman to Miss Roddam); W.M.Sillitoe, R Fleck, G Northwood, (saddler); J Cartwright, (tobacconist, sub-postmaster); H Perry, W Aston, T Trumper, J Tomlinson, W Brayne, E.F.Bennion, (printer and bookseller); W Vickers, J Hodnett, J Owen, (tailor); E Ford, R Aston, A Penson, (tailor); W Roberts, G Harris and W Taylor."

Most members were ordinary workmen, members of Friendly Societies, such as Bennion and Trumper from the Oddfellows. The St Georges Old Brass Band, who had previously played in the street, began the service with a short selection after which the Rev Provost Talbot, Rector of Church Eaton and the Rev Budgen of Newport, took their seats on the platform for the service. The collection was £12.08.04 about £3 less than the previous year. At the parish church in the evening the Rev Provost Talbot again preached and according to custom a proportion of the days collection was devoted to the fund, the churchwardens handing over £7.12.02 being £1.12.00 more than 1902. This was regarded as most satisfactory by everyone.

Henry Lunn needs a special mention as one of those devoted volunteers who have served Newport. As well as secretary of the Hospital Sunday for 32 years he was a superintendent of the church Sunday School, subscription collector for the National School, organiser of the choir outings and 21 years secretary of the Literary Institute. An excellent musician, he played a double bass bigger than himself, while his wife was a renowned pianist; he was able to form a family orchestra which, reinforced by professionals for major events, was able to entertain Newport for many years. He came to the town as a foreman printer at the Newport Advertiser, later set up his own business in the Market Square with his wife in the front premises as a fancy goods business, and then sold his business back to the Advertiser when he retired in 1914.

By 1911 it was felt interest was waning though there were still collections in town, a parade and a service. There was now further income from an unlikely source. Pat Collins the showman and fair owner came to Newport every 28 May which was the towns traditional Fair, however he had only one day and should have dismantled and gone that same night. By now fairs were huge logistical enterprises and one day was not enough to recoup the costs. Collins cleverly got round this restriction by using the fair organ for a concert and selling seats on the gondolas as a stand on the Sunday and giving the money to the hospital fund. He got his extra days, the charity got money and the authorities fumed. In 1911 the fair gave £13 from this event.

J Carrier Brown the secretary in 1924 commented that the fund which had begun in 1875 and had been in the Market Hall since 1883 should return to the church as a united service since the collection in the Market Hall was not worth moving the market stalls and the children misbehaved. In 1932 the Cottage Hospital was in being and they suggested a Saturday Fund consisting of regular payments each week to cover treatment at Stafford and Shrewsbury hospitals. This became the Hospital Sunday Committee and Saturday Fund. Many big companies such as Audley Engineering and Ashworth's timber yard gave directly to the Saturday Fund. By 1938 N.B. Saunders of Audley Engineering was chairman and income was £123.11.05 from boxes and the Sunday collections, while the Saturday Fund contributed £29.07.07. Donations were made to the Nursing Home (Roddam House), Shrewsbury Royal Infirmary, the Eye, Ear and Throat Hospital, Stafford Infirmary, the King Edward Sanatorium, (Shirlett), the local ambulance (run commercially by J.W. Danby), the Cottage Hospital, the Oakengates ambulance and the Lady Forester Convalescent Home in Llandudno.

Even after the opening of the Cottage Hospital donations were spread over a wide range of organisations and the intention was still not just to donate but to pay the travel expenses of Newport people to hospitals. At the RSI treatment was still by recommends from subscribers, so despite donations, patients still had to pay when they got to hospital.

In the 1980's the Cottage Hospital revived Hospital Sunday. Appealing for support for Sunday 18 October 1981 Gladys Smallman wrote, "When I was a little girl and after I was married, Hospital Sunday was held the first Sunday in June. Pat Collins put on an organ recital for the hospital and it was 2/6d to sit in the gondolas, while the music played and crowds of people stood to listen. Mr Aston, the cabinet maker, who lived where the Suzyanne shop now is [6 High Street], with Mr Heatley who lived in Wellington Road (his home is now demolished), arranged for the collectors and these two men gave out the vouchers for Stafford Hospital."

Mary Roddam, a wealthy lady from Edgmond, had seen through her work as a Guardian, how sickness and age were the cause of poverty and in 1893 set up the Newport Benefit Nursing Association, later called the Newport and District Nursing Association. This provided general and maternity nursing for women in their own homes. Given the "self-help" philosophy of the time the aim was "to help people help themselves and not depend upon charity" therefore treatment was for members who paid different levels of subscriptions. The money trained and provided two, later four, nurses and a matron, what were known as "cottage" or "district" nurses. By 1900 Edwardian poverty had expanded the service with the purchase of a house in Newport, known as Roddam House, and a second one next door. These were a base and a home for the nurses and were a private venture by Miss Roddam though the home and the nurses were seen as one by the townspeople.

In 1893 subscriptions were class one, 2/- pa, (78 subscribers), class two 3/- (44); by 1904 subscriptions were 2/-, 3/- and 5/-. This gave free medical treatment for a year though there were payments for such things as confinements. In 1921 the subscription was 4/6 [22½p] but there were complaints that this was too much to collect in one go and working people should be able to pay weekly in pennies and halfpennies. This feeling that the nurses were for the 'toffs' not the working women was raised often as in 1904 and 1922 this was probably inevitable where different classes of subscription gave different benefits. There was also ill feeling that some parishes donated more than other parishes, for example in 1921 Edgmond, with 913 people, gave £28 while Newport with a population of 2,800 gave £35. Even with subscriptions, donations, fundraising, Hospital Sunday and charges Miss Roddam still had deficits to make up each year from her own purse.

Though treatment was not free and universal, it is astonishing what care the Nursing Association and Roddam House was providing at the creation of the National Health Service in 1948. That year nurses dealt with nearly 5,000 visits including surgical, antenatal, maternity, medical, health and orthopaedic, together with the work of school nurses, this amounted to over 400 cases. The Home, by 1948 mainly a maternity home as County Councils had taken over welfare work, had at times included infant welfare facilities, dental and eye clinics that saved long journeys to Shrewsbury. That year Roddam House dealt with 80 maternity, mainly working class mothers, 26 midwifery, 510 antenatal examinations and 13 medical - often surgery. There were assets of £6,478 an endowment of £6,000 and an overdraft of £361. The nurses had cars. The house was sold to the County Council who continued to use it for clinical and public health purposes until 1953 when the Welfare Clinic in Beaumaris Road was built. At the sale the house had six bedrooms or wards for in-patients and four bedrooms for nurses and extensive domestic facilities.

The end was not peaceful with disputes between the Newport UDC and R.P.Liddle the solicitor, now secretary of the Association, over the application of the money. These continued until 1952 when the "Mary

Selina Roddam Aid in Sickness Fund" was set up out of the proceeds of the sale of Roddam House and the £6,000 legacy to the Nursing Association. In 1952 the Fund stood at £4,475 and was to be used to cover the poor in the parishes of Newport, Chetwynd, Church and Chetwynd Aston, Woodcote, Edgmond, Longford and Forton supplying special food and medicines, medical comforts, bedding, fuel, medical and surgical appliances, domestic help and convalescence.

Roddam House and the nurses were a pioneering movement before the welfare state and are remembered with affection and it was their ending that dismayed Newport, which was missed most and which the town felt more important than the Cottage Hospital. To understand why requires a look at the Annabelle Lady Boughey Trust.

Lady Annabelle Boughey died 18 February 1914 leaving a legacy in Trust of £15,000 to build a Cottage Hospital for Newport, £5,000 for the fabric and £10,000 as supporting investment for its upkeep, this was invested mainly in railway stock, Midland Railway, North Staffs Railway, Indian Railways and the LNWR and in War Loan Stock, ironically just before the Great War started. This philanthropic impulse was seen in every Shropshire market town for example the Lady Forester Hospitals in Broseley and Much Wenlock.

The war prevented any action and it was November 1917 before the trustees purchased 1.9 acres of land in Station Road off Beville Stanier the local MP, who had just been knighted in the June birthday honours. Income had accumulated and been put in more War Stock and there was £500 in cash but by 1920 Rev. Budgen was the only trustee remaining and Col. Sykes of Longford Hall, Capt. Foster of Woodcote and C.W.Smallman owner of the Newport Advertiser were appointed. Heavy costs had made building impossible and the trustees tried to give money to other organisations such as the Nursing Association and the ambulance but the Charity Commissioners refused, the will being very specific. They were left with the legacy and little incentive to spend it.

By 1924 the income was £750 pa and it was hoped to just use this for construction and keep the capital intact and in May 1924 tenders were invited. Unfortunately tenders came in around £13,000 well beyond the intention of the trustees and by 25 February 1926 they were at Stafford Assizes defending a claim for costs from their architect Frank Hearne. He was awarded £69. In June 1927 tenders were out again with new architects Edmund Kirby and Sons of Liverpool. The contract for a 14 bed hospital went to Henry Price and Sons of Shrewsbury.

Compared to other Cottage Hospitals in the county Newport was late on the scene and the concept of small local hospitals was declining, many feeling that there was no need for them, the existing facilities being sufficient. These facilities were Roddam House with its maternity and clinical facilities; the comforting and ever present District Nurses; funds for travel to district hospitals and faster motor transport and roads to get there. Industry was subsidising its workers and the County Council, formed in 1888, was playing an increasing role in health and welfare work, providing funds for the voluntary sector such as the Nursing Associations and clinics like Roddam.

This reluctance to support the Cottage Hospital was seen in a meeting of Newport Urban District Council 12 November 1927. The council was fearful that income would not be enough to support the hospital and that they would be asked for financial assistance. Cllr C.W.Smallman, a hospital trustee, "understood" people thought it would be a white elephant in that it only had 8 (?) beds and could not be self-supporting he also believed there would only be £600-700 a year for upkeep and the Nursing Association needed that already and still made a deficit. The hospital would need at least £200 pa more and people got tired of appeals and entertainments for raising money. The legacy would be better used for an ambulance but the Charity Commissioners had forbidden this. Cllr E.J.Wright also wanted an ambulance to reach the county hospitals and thought the idea of a hospital had been dropped. He too believed it would be a millstone around their necks for years. Cllr A.O.Talbot thought the hospital would be redundant and might have been alright in the days of slow moving traffic and suggested the purchase of the Rectory (then at Beaumaris House) and combining it with Roddam House. The bequest he believed was too "cast iron". The unanimous opinion of the Council was that the hospital would be a "white elephant".

These were not lightweight critics but to be fair the tags of "white elephant" and "millstone" have been applied by similar people to later successful developments such as the Cosy Hall and the Guildhall. They usually hide a fear of involvement.

A more telling objection came from Tom Collins the ex-headmaster of Adams' Grammar School in a letter of November 1930. Supporting the hospital he said its main fault was that the very poor would not be admissible because they could not pay; it was, he felt, more like a nursing home than a general hospital.

By 1930 the role of these voluntary, charitable, hospitals was already being questioned nationally. There were 56,000 of them requiring re-organisation and rationalisation, unable to survive on donations and fees from patients yet fearful of losing their independence by applying for public finance.

The hospital was opened with a golden key on 16 May 1930 by Viscount Bridgeman and the Rev Budgen, who by this time had retired. Also present were the Bishop of Lichfield, Dame Agnes Hunt, Col. Sykes and Mrs Morris of Aqualate. The story has it that when Lord Bridgeman went to open the door it stuck and he could not get it open. Lord Bradford told him to put his foot through the glass!

The building had cost £12,000 paid for from income, the original £15,000 still being intact. There was a management committee of 18 who were also trustees, one from the Newport Urban District Council and one from Newport Rural District Council which was abolished in 1936. Donors of £20 were life members and could give two recommendations a year; subscribers of 10/6 one recommendation for each 10/6; single donations of not less than £3 by individual or groups were allowed one recommendation for each 15/-. Recommendations could only be given to anyone not able to pay full maintenance fees and would give the holder six days treatment in a general ward for half fees while a holder of two recommendations would have six days free. The scale of fees was - general ward, 4/- per day, 2 bed ward, 7/6, single ward 10/6 per day. All medical costs were determined between the doctors and the patients, the beds being for local general practitioner use. The category of "subscribers" could dispense their recommendations to anyone they liked, giving 12/- value on every 10/6 subscribed the minimum charge being 4/- per day.

Accidents occurring outside Newport were charged 10/6 a day Messrs Hodge, Harriss and Elliott, solicitors, being billed for £5.18.06 in October 1938 for eight days treatment for one of their clients injured in a motor accident.

In 1932 more subscribers were being sought and it was suggested that recommendations be pooled allowing poorer people to be treated in the large general wards leaving the smaller wards to those who could pay. In 1936 there were complaints that many recommends in private hands were never used so that people who were sick could not get into hospital and it was urged that subscribers with unused recommends donate them to the hospital for treating poorer patients. One could see the point Tom Collins was making.

There were frequent deficits, £24 in 1932 and £351 in 1937. The first Hospital Ball in February 1934 in the Town Hall raised £40 but this was shared with the Roddam Home. In 1935 to celebrate the Kings Jubilee Mr and Mrs Edkins from Arlington House donated two electric globes for the gate pillars but with World War II donations dried up from the carnival, Harper Adams' Rag Day and other sources. H. Ford from Lilleshall Hall became chairman having given £100. Miss Perry, the first matron, thought the war had little effect on life in the hospital "..we remained in Newport and it didn't really affect us a great deal. We didn't have any casualties." However, life was not always smooth a squabble among the doctors in July 1940 requiring meetings and a resort to referees to settle what became a most unpleasant affair.

At the beginning there were two wards with 4 beds, male and female; two wards with 2 beds, male and female and two private wards. Staff slept in. Miss Perry was the first matron until 1948, retiring with the advent of the National Health Service; a former RSI nurse she had trained in the operating theatre and was proficient in massage and X-rays, the hospital having facilities for both. In 1932 there had been 95 residents, 43 operations done by local GP's such as Dr George Elkington and visiting surgeons such as Mr Sworn of Stafford and Mr Cookson; 52 X-rays and 116 various treatments though there was no general outpatients department. In 1936 there were 169 residents over the year, 102 operations, 121 X-rays and 315 general. Many of the wounded came from the adjacent Ashworth's timber yard and in the season from the nearby cricket ground.

With the advent of the National Health Service on 5 July 1948 the Cottage Hospital was transferred to Group 22 (Stafford) of the Birmingham Regional Hospital Board. At the last meeting of the management committee of which the Rev. Bradley was chairman, F Bird (Audley Engineering) secretary and R.J.Davies (Davies, White and Perry) treasurer, it was confirmed that the endowment fund was not transferable to the State, Lady Boughey having made the condition that if the hospital became chargeable on, or supported by, public funds, the income from the endowment was to be applied to other charitable purposes the trustees thought fit. Application had been made to the Charity Commissioners to this end. Meanwhile £400 was handed over to the Roddam Nursing home to make them safe for twelve months until they too closed down.

Thursday 18 May 1950 was the first meeting of the new Lady Boughey Charity to co-opt members under the new constitution now separated from the hospital. Some of the original trustees, according to diaries of the time, "...not much liking the sound of some of the new members."

Under a Charity Commission Scheme of January 1951 the funds were placed in the Charity of Annabelle Lady Boughey which after applying funds at their discretion including a pension of £312 to Miss Perry former matron, the balance went to the Lady Boughey and Mary Roddam Housing Trust. By 1975 the same body of trustees were managing the former nursing fund, the sickness fund, the former hospital money and the Roddam Housing Trust. The benevolence of Annabelle Boughey and Mary Roddam had come together and is serving the poor, sick and homeless long after the hospital has ceased.

There were early problems, the hospital being closed all July 1949 because of staff shortages and holidays, but Miss Underwood, a nurse until 1969, emphasised "There were no great changes, we got on well under the Stafford Hospital management and then later under Shrewsbury". The hospital was costing £6,275 to run or £12 per week per patient in December 1952; it had 7 beds with an average of 7 patients a day with an average stay of 15 days; it dealt with 250 X-rays and 2,616 casualties; tonsils and adenoids were done and the local doctors still retained use of the beds for their cases. It was not felt any major alterations were needed.

The supporters of Newport Cottage Hospital and cottage hospitals in general became increasingly anxious after 1963 and the creation of Telford, formerly Dawley, New Town which was estimated to increase in population from 74,000 in 1968 to 135,000 in 1999. Cosford Hospital, a RAF establishment but used by the local population particularly accident cases on the A41, closed and there began the agitation for a district hospital in Telford. Added to this was the not unreasonable assumption that the Area Health Authority had no money to improve or expand the cottage hospital even if it had the political will, so it is understandable that in 1974 the League of Friends of the Cottage Hospital was formed as a charity to maintain and improve facilities as a first step in its survival. Suspicions increased in September 1979 when the Regional Health Authority submitted an outline planning application to build six dwellings on the hospital site to make it more attractive to developers. Town councillors totally rejected the scheme though they had no planning powers. By 1983 the League had raised over £64,000 to build a new 4 bed women's ward, a new outpatients department, bed replacements, new bathrooms, X-ray and physiotherapy equipment, numerous other items and assistance with salaries.

Newport Cottage Hospital

In response to the consultation document on Telford Hospital in October 1983 while welcoming the proposal to keep the minor injuries service, the outpatients department, the radiography, physiotherapy and certain consultant clinics the Friends objected to the plan to reserve all the 18 beds in Newport for geriatric use, they strenuously maintained that it should remain a Community Hospital with the local GP's allocating the beds as they had always done "effectively and efficiently". The district hospital they thought should complement not replace the cottage hospital.

The Shropshire Health Authority issued a document "Caring for the Elderly" in 1982 and another consultation document in January 1988 from which point the writing was on the wall. Newport hospital was one of the hospitals proposed for closure. 205 patients had been treated at the hospital in 1986, with an average stay of 29 days, the average age of patients being 78 years the most common diagnoses being heart failure, stroke and chest disease. There were 17 beds available for general practitioner use. A total of 28 outpatient clinics had been held at which 259 outpatients were seen 109 being new cases. There were 6,916 minor casualties of which 2,758 were new.

Under the proposals, general acute work would be transferred to Telford and continuing care and rehabilitation to Shifnal. All outpatients would go to Telford where there would be full accident and emergency facilities. It was understood that local GP`s would provide some minor casualty services but the hospital would cease to exist unless taken over by the private sector, the local authority or an independent trust. The closure of Newport would save £322,000 in running costs and the sale of all the redundant sites in Shropshire would bring in £1.7m none of which would be available to be spent on the cottage hospitals whatever their future role in the community. Newport would close in June 1989 with admissions stopping a month earlier.

Protests, as in the other market towns affected, were not new as we have seen with the setting up of the League of Friends and in 1977 a public meeting in the church under the auspices of the Rev J.C.Hill at which a member of the audience suggesting he would prefer to be treated at a modern hospital at Telford rather than Newport Cottage Hospital, was howled down. Today twenty years on (2010), such a statement would be seen as a matter of fact and not "outrageous". Action packs were prepared and protest cards printed and groups and individuals were encouraged to write to health officials, MP`s, Health Ministers and Mrs Thatcher. Union was sought with League of Friends in other towns for joint action. The outrage and the shock took the customary forms the Mayor calling a meeting with John Biffen MP; an action group was formed and officials elected; a huge public meeting met in the Burton Borough School; an open day was held at the hospital and one lovely November morning townspeople flocked to the cause and linked arms, led by the Mayor, all around the hospital. The Mayor joined a delegation of all Shropshire mayors led by Mr Biffen, to meet the Health Minister, Mr John Newton, in the House of Commons, and at the Civic Ball 1988 he raised the banner of "no money, no hospital, no vote" though there is no evidence that anyone changed their party allegiance over the cause. John Biffen former Leader of the House and MP for Shropshire North, which then included Newport, stated "To take away ten rural hospitals in a very rural county is to totally unbalance the provision of health services."

Interested groups struggled to be seen on the right side of the protest, the League of Friends made sure the chairmanship of the Action Committee was theirs; the political parties made sure committee officials were shared out - the Conservatives offered a nearly new shop, if one could be found, the Liberals a promise to print cards - and at the hand linking around the hospital there were political scuffles to make sure they were seen on the photographs. Despite this behaviour, as the Newport Advertiser said, it was the grassroots gut feeling expressed by ordinary people, who were usually silent, that marked the fight.

Behind all the controversy wiser heads were coming to a more realistic conclusion, the hospital was closing, the banners, the marches, the furious letters, the nostalgic appeals to a past that had never existed were pointless. The closure was not a short term effect of the building of a new hospital at Telford it was a deeply entrenched national financial change, it was the relentless growth of demand in an ageing population, it was the need for fundamental change in administration as health entered a highly technical and scientific age, it was the need to find another role for cottage hospitals, to prove they had a function in these changing times. As one writer put it 6 November 1987 "We must get away from the vague, flag waving demand that the Cottage Hospital must remain. We must find an alternative programme which people can work for even if the worst happens." He suggested the hospital become an administrative, consultative, information centre for all welfare services; for District Nurses; home helps; X-ray, physiotherapy; child welfare, ante-natal; day centre for the elderly with provision for bathing and chiropody, a complete change in the traditional view of a cottage hospital.

The worst happened, the hospital closed in December 1989 and the discussion became one of ownership of the buildings and their future use. As early as July 1986 the League of Friends were asking for the return of the buildings at a nominal rent and suggesting a residential home on the site and the retention of X-ray, physiotherapy and hospital beds for GP`s. The Health Authority appeared to support this agreeing to the establishment of an Independent Trust for Newport and that the building "could" be leased at a peppercorn rent provided, and note the proviso, "suitable proposals were submitted." Newport took this as a definite promise that the property would be handed back to the town but in October 1990 it was clear the Authority were thinking of selling at a figure of half a million pounds or a rental of £30,000 a year. The headlines expressed shock and horror and the belief the town had been betrayed for commercial gain.

The reply was the Newport (Shropshire) Community Hospital Trust incorporated on 10 May 1990 and registered as a charity on the 20 December 1990, being amended in January 1993 and 30 August 2005. It became the Cottage Hospital Trust then the Cottage Care Centre Trust Ltd classified for general charitable purposes for elderly and old people with disabilities.

Between 1990 and 1992 the Trust drew up plans in consultation with the Health Authority to provide a community hospital on the site containing the transferred clinic from Beaumaris Road, physiotherapy and X-ray facilities, the latter paid for by the League of Friends, a day care centre for hospice and respite care and a minimum 10 bed in-patient facility for short term respite-rehabilitation-hospice care. This had involved purchasing the site from the Authority for £225,000 the final payment of £100,000 being due in March 1995. It was estimated that £350,000 would be needed to set up the in-patient facility and that the running costs for the first year would be £150,000 a total of £500,000 needing to be raised. 1992 was declared "The Year of the Hospital Trust" and a high profile fund raising committee was set up and an appeal launched throughout the town. Donations included a legacy of over £40,000, £30,000 from the Boughey Trust and £160,000 from the Community Fund (National Lottery).

In a letter of October 1994 the Chairman of what was now the "Cottage Hospital Trust" outlined the progress made. The Trust was responsible for the management and maintenance of the hospital building and its activities. The Day Centre had opened on 3 May 1994 providing in addition, chiropody, hair care, bathing, lunches and free transport. Over £100,000 had been spent mainly on regulations as regards fire and health and safety. Most of this was financed through the activities of the League of Friends and their shop in Baddeley Court. The Friends directly financed the X-ray unit in excess of £10,000 pa. From May 1999 to May 2005 the Friends raised over £370,000 and spent £286,000. The Trust between April 1999 and March 2005 had a gross income of £1,105,360 and total expenditure of £934,957.

Today (2010) the Cottage Care Centre is on the original hospital site but much changed as the occasion has necessitated. It contains a Day Centre, nursery, X-ray and physiotherapy, welfare and commercial offices. The respite beds never materialised. The day centre lounge has been extended and new bathing and kitchen facilities added, there is new office accommodation; a new porch and conservatory; there is a sit out area and newly laid out gardens and extra land for its extensive car parking. The X-ray department was refurbished in 2008 paid for by public appeal and two new accessible buses were purchased through grants and fundraising.

From 1848 you could travel by train to hospital in Shrewsbury and Stafford but emergencies still entailed a painful journey by road, on the 12 September 1895, Margaret Simpson, daughter of the local chimney sweep, was badly scalded in a boiling vat of beer at the Wharf Tavern in Water Lane despite her terrible burns she had to be conveyed in a cab to Stafford where she died. Most public houses and undertakers could provide ambulances and after 1894 the new Urban and Rural District Councils, Oakengates, Shifnal, Dawley, Wellington and Newport Rural and Urban, all had such private arrangements.

In August 1929 the first motor ambulance in Newport was on view made available through the efforts of another Friendly Society the Royal and Ancient and Order of Buffalos, the "Buffs". They organised a "Daisy Day" where they sold daisies which with donations, raised £19.19.06 for the ambulance fund. In 1935 Danby of the Greyhound was running an ambulance at 6d a mile or 2/6 for a local journey; this was used by Newport Rural Council. Newport UDC also used this ambulance which was later run by Stanworth of the Old Bell. During the war Civil Defence also ran an ambulance with 2 drivers and 3 attendants all working in the town. Between 1945 and 1948 all these strands had to be disentangled.

In May 1945 the Urban District Council discussed a joint scheme to pool the ambulances of the local councils to create a fleet of 3-4 ambulances centred at Oakengates with a full time driver and mechanic, at the same time they were approached by Mr Abbot who had run the Civil Defence scheme during the war to continue with that service with the existing personnel. Typically the Council decided to continue discussing the first option while pursuing the second. Of course they chose neither deciding to stick with the private arrangement with Stanworth at the Bell. Undaunted a public meeting agreed to buy the Civil Defence ambulance for £50 and proceed with the scheme of Mr Abbot using the old fire station in St Marys Street as a base.

It was decided to put the scheme in operation with Mr Abbott as secretary and Rev. D.H.Davies from the Congregational Church as Chairman. They appealed for funds and agreed to purchase up to £15 worth of Civil Defence equipment from the County. The initial cost of the scheme was estimated at £100 with an annual cost of £80. The service was for all whether they could pay or not, to cover Newport and local parishes. It would be operated by former members of the Civil Defence providing employers were willing to let personnel go during working hours. G.S Whitting was the chief driver. George Strettle Whitting was an advisory agricultural economist aged 31 in 1946 when he was elected to the UDC. A First Aider and member of Toc H he had raised large sums for charity during the war and obviously believed he could do it again.

The opening ceremony took place at 3 pm on Saturday 8 December 1945 in a roped area in the Square with a loudspeaker. Miss Perry the hospital matron performed the ceremony and the ambulance was open for inspection till dusk. A house to house collection was taken the next week. They also promoted popular ambulance dances at the Market Hall with Ken Whiteley and his band, admission 4/-. Between this date and February 1946 the ambulance was used on 8 occasions clocking up 464 miles.

Newport Voluntary Ambulance Workers

The UDC was in a quandary faced with the County Council and its obligation to create a county wide service and the local voluntary scheme. The county scheme would involve £120 on the rates plus 6d a mile and 3/6 for waiting also charges would be based on rateable value not population which meant Newport would pay more. On the other hand the voluntary scheme would be free! The thought of having to pay always made Councils dither and in December 1946 the UDC was still hoping the County Council would recognise the voluntary scheme which would relieve them of having to make a decision. While not convinced the voluntary service would answer the needs of Newport the UDC still went ahead and let the old fire station in St Marys Street to the volunteers at 5/- per week plus rates while themselves using Stanworth's bus.

The County Council had a duty to set up a county wide ambulance service by 1948 which would replace the existing seventeen ambulance authorities in Shropshire of which the County was one with four vehicles. By July 1948 the County Council had made it clear it would not support Newport and built a depot at Donnington for four vehicles. Local GP's and the Medical Officer of Health, were not wholeheartedly in favour of the voluntary scheme, Dr Elkington on one trip to Shrewsbury being stranded in the ambulance during a snowstorm with just a shovel. More importantly by April 1946 there was a serious lack of volunteer drivers between 9am and 4pm normal working hours and the group approached the UDC to see if one of their employees, Mr W Steventon, could be released to cover those hours. Another disadvantage was that the ambulance was twelve years old.

When the County scheme came in officially in July 1948 the volunteers objected and so did the UDC, despite the fact that it had prevaricated so long, with petitions to the Ministry of Health. The volunteer ambulance was officially closed at 3pm on Saturday 10 July 1948 having been called out 376 times and travelled 13,902 miles, one case every two days. At the time of the closure the ambulance was actually on its last journey between Newport and Gobowen. The credit balance of £74 was distributed to charities. The agitation over the ambulance was a foretaste of that for the Cottage Hospital forty years later.

After 1948 Roddam House, Hospital Sunday and the local ambulance service disappeared partly because in the 1920's the County Council which had increasingly subsidised existing organisations began to provide such welfare and medical services directly on a more efficient regional level. District nursing, midwifery, school medical and dental treatment and ambulances came under the County Council and their first Welfare Centre was actually opened in Beaumaris Road Newport in 1953. The war showed how inadequate local services were to national problems and emergencies, not just in health but in areas like fire protection, local volunteer brigades being effectively nationalised in 1940.

Though the cottage hospital did good work between 1948 and 1988 its survival was the result of the time it took for the NHS to replace the Victorian hospital system it inherited, when it did the cottage hospitals would go or a new role for them found. It was a question of time.

This new role was achieved and nurtured by the hard core group of Trustees and Friends who were there twenty years ago many others at the original pomp having melted away. Today what does remain is the generosity - £50,000 is required each year - the volunteers - the Henry Lunns - the community spirit which sustain the Trust and its community objectives just as they sustained Hospital Sunday, the District Nurses and Roddam House over one hundred years ago.

It All Fell Down.

It may be useful before we start on the "Tuckers" episode to describe the wider context. 1990 was the year base rates peaked at 15% and the property market collapsed. Large and small got caught, the Church Commissioners for example losing £400m in property speculation. Then there was English Heritage an organisation originally set up to protect the English landscape which had become overwhelmed by listed buildings and demands from aristocratic stately homes, so that a whole "heritage industry" had later grown up with money from the Heritage Lottery Fund. Tuckers was also a listed building but how important historically was open to debate having been altered over the years while the façade was Regency tacked on to the original. Nobody knew what the arch at the side was, it was an intrusion with no historical pedigree though people clamoured for its retention. However once a building is listed it is an offence to demolish, alter or extend without going through a complicated, time-consuming process.

Small developers had a tendency to pack up and go away or let the property fall down leaving the local authority as the last stop. Even with grants and tax concessions there would be no profit in development and it would be left to the Local Authority to confiscate or compulsory purchase. Wrekin District Council already had an example of what could happen, for across its boundary North Shropshire District had had to acquire Pell Wall Hall, designed by Sir John Sloane, for one pound. The developer and people like Liz and John Mason, were caught between the economic recession, the heritage bureaucracy and the planning bureaucracy and such a situation can seriously damage your wealth if not your health.

When Tucker's shop in Newport High Street fell down on Thursday 3 August 1989 there were many who knew it would happen. "I am a layman" said one 'expert', "but even I could see there was something wrong with the building." They recalled years afterwards how the collapse was inevitable and how they had never walked under the tunnel of scaffolding that covered the pavement preferring to trust the other side of the street by the Barley Mow. Hindsight apart, the mess had to be cleared up and the posturing of the politicians, the use of it by the political parties to beat each other with rhetoric, and the local newspaper's soundbite of "The shame of Newport", achieved nothing. The only solution was seen by some and quietly accepted and worked on. By 1994 no developer, with property speculation discredited, was going to come to the rescue.

At a town council meeting that year Malcolm Miles pointed out that the then Wrekin District Council had set a precedent in other parts of the district by buying up empty property by compulsory purchase and the same could be done with the Tuckers site. "In my eyes there have always been just two solutions to the problem. Firstly, that Wrekin Council should buy the property and market it or develop it themselves if no buyer was found. Or, secondly, a business person or consortium of businessmen from the town should band together to buy and redevelop it." He knew that the second option was impossible though a member of the Chamber of Commerce offered to head a consortium to buy the site "even if we only put up a façade". They might shout about the effect on their business but there was no commercial base in the town capable of providing the capital and the initiative. He was correct, and slowly, though derided, local government provided the answer, though today it hurts many to accept that this option succeeded.

The value, the scale, the opulence of a building increases as you near the commercial heart of a town and this is true in Newport. The Tucker building on the west of the High Street opposite the market square and the church, reflected its expensive position. It had a frontage of nearly 70 feet, was three storied with a depth going back to Beaumaris Road. It was near the main coaching inn of the town the Red Lion, now Barclays Bank.

The Blakemores who lived there, were a prosperous business family, Thomas Blakemore being a linen draper in 1790, while his son, another Thomas and his daughter, Mary Anne, continued as drapers, mercers, woolstaplers, that is dealers and sorters of wool, and also maltsters. In 1831 they converted the malthouse into a mercers and drapers shop lighting it with their own gas house and gasholder at the rear. With its lighting and battlements and the dazzling array of goods, they promised "to astonish the natives." They had property along the High Street near Adams House, where after her marriage Mary Anne went to live, as well as a warehouse in Bakehouse Lane (Stafford Street). The house next door to the shop housed the family, 6 apprentices and journeyman, 3 female servants and 1 male servant. John Warner who took over the business in 1846 had an equally substantial household and the house was to later take his name "Warner House". These apprentices and assistants in the attics and garrets of such buildings were a lively feature of the town and were not beyond placing planks from one attic bedroom to the one next door in order to sneak out and play cards. Demolition also removed some of the scurrilous graffiti which adorned their bedroom walls!

The 1867 "to let" notice reveals a shop 14` high, 62` long and 18` wide with two large plate glass windows, a skylight in the centre, and cellars and a large warehouse, a hat room, a bonnet and ribbon room and the main feature a wonderful staircase under a gothic arch, the shop being handsomely fitted out with fixtures and counters. Writing in 2000 Jeremy Tucker believed no 55, the shop, had been a chapel until the early nineteenth century and that organ pipes had been where the gothic arch was. No 53 was a splendid town house with a frontage of 69` with fifteen bedrooms and two attics and water closets. There were three reception rooms some of which were later converted to showrooms, two kitchens, pantries and cellars that probably held workshops. A large staircase was illuminated by a lantern window and the front doorway was ornamented with a pillared porch in the Roman Doric style. The windows were around the late 18th century with a wide central light flanked by two narrower ones with sashes. There were elaborate side pillars, a frieze and cornice around the windows. In the magnificent garden was, and still is, an icehouse. Indeed 53 was a fine, elegant town residence.

The house and business had various tenants but until 1897 remained in the ownership of John Warner's daughters Martha and Sarah who lived off the considerable property of their father. They left Newport with their mother and lived in Italy then London where Sarah died, aged 87 in 1933 and Martha aged 94, in 1938. They were generous to Newport Church and the altar and lectern in the cemetery chapel were purchased through them.

Samuel Smith, who had the ironmongers business next door at 57 High Street, bought the house and shop and named the house "Warner House". In 1900 he turned the front of the house into a shop, with new plate glass windows. He was a prominent man in the business, social and political life of the town and only left in 1905 to go to Australia for the health of his daughter Ida. This must have worked because she was still writing from Queensland in 1951. The house continued to be rented out as a drapers and the ironmongers shop, no. 55, was bought by John Tucker of Adcote Manor, Gloucester.

An advertisement in May 1905 announced "J Tucker general furnishing and agricultural ironmongers, electrician, gas, hot water and sanitary engineers, The Square, Newport, Salop, having recently purchased the ironmongery business for many years carried on by Mr Samuel Smith…." By 1907 he had an engineering department in Stafford Street for agricultural equipment, mowers, oil, gas and petrol engines and was lighting the shop with petrol-air gas lighting. John came to Newport with his wife and his sister Elizabeth who died aged 96 at Warner House in October 1980. Unfortunately John separated from his wife and the family was cared for by May Barlow who became the companion of John and to whom he left the High Street property. May died in May 1997. By 1929 John is listed at 53 and 55 High Street though the front of Warner House continued to be leased as a drapers, between 1904 and 1928 by Arthur William Clarke and between 1928 and 1947 by J.S.Wheeler, though still trading as Clarke's.

When John Tucker retired in 1942 his son Herbert took over the Newport business and expanded and diversified though he always indicated he was an ironmonger first and a businessman second and this was the reason for the continuance of traditional, uneconomic, lines with modern developments. Old stock was never discarded. Visiting the ironmongery was like stepping into the past an adventure back in history accompanied by smells of paraffin, paint, disinfectant and numerous oils. A shop where screws were bought by the pint, nails by the pound, methylated spirits by the bottle and putty was weighed and wrapped in newspaper. Whiting was sold like footballs and galvanised goods lined the pavement outside. Obscure items were fetched out of Edwardian drawers and shelves to satisfy the most outdated and peculiar requests. Deliveries were made to and from the High Street and paraffin loaded onto vans for rural customers the same way.

When Herbert was born the family lived at what is now the Veterinary Surgery in Newport High Street and by the time he joined the business in 1927 there were branches at Oswestry and Shrewsbury and in the former he ran a sports outfitters and gunsmiths. Herbert was an outdoor man, cricket and golf, shooting and coursing and particularly hockey. He was an active townsman, councillor, Rotarian and a Freemason. He died in August 1988 and his son Jeremy concentrated the business in the Stafford Street premises. This closed in 1997.

Tuckers was physically at the heart of the town; its buildings were part of its heritage; it had served the community over eighty years in a unique way, as its owners had served the town over three generations. It embodied a solid, dependable, comforting quality. Its collapse in 1989 was not just a physical loss it was the destruction of a whole community experience and therefore an even greater shock. But this was the time of the speculator, the developer, the time when any project, however speculative, was bound to make a profit.

Unstable the building certainly was, the contractor clearing interior walls undermining a central chimney stack to create a larger, open, show area, which brought the building down in spectacular fashion on a hot August morning. John Mason maintains the engineer and the contractors did not understand the basic construction of a box frame building and no matter how elegant the frontages most buildings in the High Street of Newport were eighteenth century facades tacked on to earlier wooden structures. The timbers fanned out from central chimney stacks interlocking with the wall timbers with timbers on the next floor laid crossways to the lower floor and so on, giving a tight, interdependent frame which could move and breathe. Mess with one section and the whole could be in peril.

The collapse of Tuckers

Thursday was fortunate because although most businesses had ceased to observe half-day closing the town was still traditionally quiet on that day. As with the death of President Kennedy people can still remember what they were doing on that lovely morning.

Just after 11am Tucker's ironmongery collapsed into Newport High Street leaving scaffolding and debris across the road resembling the wartime blitz. Shoppers and passers-by rushed to help and lift the scaffolding and masonry, fearing casualties but none of the eleven workmen in the building employed by W.P.Eccleston of Oswestry, the contractor, were hurt and no passing vehicles were damaged. The area was evacuated and the High Street sealed off from Salters Lane to Wellington Road with fears of fractured gas mains. Barriers were put across St Mary's Street and no vehicles were allowed to enter the High Street unless permitted by the police. All shops and businesses were closed and evacuated as far up as Woolworths, Barclay's Bank, the Barley Mow and Boots. Staff were left wondering what to do and where to go. It was after 3.30pm before St Mary's Street was opened to traffic and pedestrians while workers and fireman continued to dismantle the scaffolding and clear the rubble. 27 fireman and five engines were involved.

There were injuries though miraculously few, Mr George Barnes, an elderly man from the Riddings, Gnosall, was taken to the intensive unit at Stafford with a broken leg and serious head and chest injuries. It was not until late October that he came out of intensive care by then he had lost a leg and an eye through the accident and his whole quality of life had gone. His house had to be altered to accommodate his injuries. Also injured by falling masonry was Mrs Stella Davies of Victoria Park, Newport. An hour after the collapse firemen were still searching the rubble but no one else was found.

Firefighters searching the rubble

Reactions to the accident differed one lady saying "lets hope it keeps the hospital open." The cottage hospital was under threat at the time. A workman was concerned that a treasure trove had been lost forever, this consisting of a bottle hidden by a Harry Duddleston in 1860. Strangely a Harry Duddleston took over the drapery business in February 1903; was this the same man?

Now the ten years saga began and the various parties took up their positions. Perhaps at this point we ought to list them: the developers, building contractor, Wrekin District Council, English Heritage, insurers and the mortgagees; add to these the public utilities water etc and perhaps others. In September 1989 English Heritage visited the site since from 1978 it was a listed building and made it plain they would resist demolition preferring some form of rebuilding on the original plan and the original façade. Any redevelopment would require special planning permission. The public and the traders, alleging loss of trade, were becoming uneasy, the site was an eyesore, uncleared, walls wobbling, rats, and protected by a hoarding that jutted out into the pavement while the adjacent building, Mason's butchers, was cracked and shored up with timber. People were looking for someone to blame.

In September 1989 at the first meeting of the Town Council since the building collapsed one councillor urged members to ask questions, not to sit back and be thankful the incident had not been worse. It was not enough to be relieved that the traffic was running normally, that the building was "now safe" and nobody had been killed. "Something happened in our town. Now we must ask how and why it happened, what has been learned and how we can make sure it never happens again."

In November 1989 it was revealed that the contractors were to be prosecuted at Telford magistrates court for "...failing to ensure that the public were not exposed to risks to their safety", but this was deferred until April 1990. It was not until June 1991 that Ecclestons were fined under health and safety regulations though they denied the charges. Meanwhile First Foundation, the owners and developers, were suing the engineer and the contractors as a third party.

By March 1990 a plan had been submitted to Wrekin District Council which preserved the original façade and proposed three shops. By now English Heritage were blaming the Council for delays for it was becoming apparent that it was impossible to reconcile the requirement of heritage and conservation with an economically viable solution. In April 1990 the developers and owners, First Foundation Property Ltd of London, submitted a proposal to restore the frontage and build two shops which would be occupied by two national chain stores. They had already received an interim bill for the costs of the collapse such as traffic diversions and safety measures. They too were blaming the local authority for planning delays.

179

Meanwhile the chairman of the Chamber of Commerce was firing off letters to everybody about the dangerous condition of the building, so many, that the County Road Engineer accused him of "verbal diarrhoea" and causing "a lot of fuss about nothing." An editorial in the local paper complained that the authorities were impotent and that only heavy fines on the developer would suffice. After a year Wrekin District had agreed plans but nothing moved because the difficulties lay in the details attached to any permission designed to reconcile the expectations for the site from the different interested parties.

John Mason, the neighbour most affected, was more direct It was, he said, unrealistic to save the lot as English Heritage wanted, "what people want to see is a front to the building in keeping with the whole street". He did not believe the site was historically that important. What English Heritage wanted was unacceptable to the owners and the attempts by the council to reconcile the differences through planning, was not helping. As time went on John was losing trade in his butchers shop with people still refusing to walk on his side of the road while because of safety he had had to leave his house. He wanted English Heritage and Wrekin Council "to get their act together".

By November 1990 there were rumours that First Foundation was selling the site. They denied this but made it plain that the refusal to allow demolition was preventing progress and even if the site was cleared there was nobody to carry out the work and it could be years before anything was resolved. Though two national drugstores were interested no development would be considered until the shop deals were clinched. While some progress had been made, Mason's dividing wall had been made safe and the insurance claim settled, nothing would happen until tenants for the two proposed shops had been found: "in the current economic climate tenants will have to be found prior to commencement". Here was the truth, the property market had collapsed, and it was no use looking to the private developer for answers. Another way would have to be found for Tuckers.

Tuckers was a microcosm, a little example of what was happening in the big world of property development in the late 1980's. Banks and institutional investors such as the insurance companies and pension funds, were lending developers an avalanche of credit while the developers themselves simply followed the practice of developing someone else's site with someone else's money. All was well if a tenant or a buyer could be found at a price high enough to pay off the banks and leave a margin of profit. If not banks could only get their money back from the particular development not the total assets of the developer. When tenants did not appear buildings were sold at a loss and the developer was ruined and all the subsidiary bodies with him. The site was left to rot and development mistakes cannot be hidden, they remain visible for decades and even generations. This happened with Tuckers.

By August 1994 the mood was pessimistic about the future of the site and people were pleased with minor steps forward such as the clearing of the pavement of rubble and the erection of a substantial hoarding to disguise the site. Though some, as usual, moaned about vandalism, the hoarding was decorated by local children with views of the town and remained the one pleasant, and undisturbed feature for years. There were other eyesores in the town but not as prominent as this from whichever direction you approached the centre. Wrekin District Council had begun negotiations to buy the site under a compulsory purchase order but acknowledged that this would be a long process. They also commissioned a development brief for the site including an artists impression showing the arch as a central entrance between the two shops and began a consultation process on what people wanted there. In 1995 a compulsory purchase order was finally applied and after a public inquiry the Council announced the official takeover of the building in May 1997. The "Advertiser" abandoned its "Shame of Newport" logo.

Community painted hoardings

181

Wrekin District Council bought the property off the Crown to which it had reverted when all concerned had walked away. First Foundation were asset strippers and by 1995 hade got rid of all other assets leaving 53/55 the only property in their portfolio.

This still left English Heritage, mortgagees and insurers to contend with. WDC continued to invite outside developers and it was not until July 1997 that the first contractor looked at demolition and it was only in the August that demolition began of the walls and chimney still standing. At this point the Masons handed over the keys to the entrance to nos. 53 and 55.

After further negotiations permission was granted for redevelopment to Derngate Holdings and in 1999 the first stone was laid to bring fifteen new homes to the site through the Beth Johnson Housing Association with a mix of maisonettes, flats and bungalows. The ground floor premises fronting the High Street became a new library at a cost of £400,000. The design incorporated residential and commercial properties combining new and old features. The library was a welcome public asset while the housing brought people back to live on the High Street.

Through English Heritage and public pressure old features were retained some, like the icehouse, previously unseen. This seventeenth century feature in the rear garden with a yew tree growing over it was discovered during the initial ground work. The Gothic stone arch whose use and origin no one has really determined was a much more obvious feature and was restored and incorporated in the design having been taken down with great difficulty one Sunday in January 1995. Building materials were also recovered and reused. Perhaps more important historically was retaining the development within the original plot so that the narrow, medieval burgage plan stretching from the High Street to Beaumaris Road will continue. So after nearly ten years something pleasing and purposeful had risen from the rubble and the grief.

Distress there was for one man who suffered most from the dreadful decade. John Mason had a prosperous butchers shop next door at number 51 High Street, a substantial building known as Weston House. Its history was as long as that of Warner House being, in 1797 a Ladies School run by Elizabeth and Jane Bennet. Elizabeth was still there in 1851 aged 88, unmarried, a proprietor of land, served by a companion, a coachman and two female servants. Edward Weston, hence the name of the house, had a pawnbroking and general dealers business until 1868 when it reverted to a Ladies School under Elizabeth and Jane Collier who had formerly had a school at Penkridge. The building was large enough to house twenty girls plus staff. When they left in 1882 the education connection continued with Mr Drennan a master at the Grammar School running a boarding establishment for pupils. Dr Baddeley lived there from 1889 and when he left in 1900 it was taken over by E.W.Mason who moved from 83 High Street trading as W.H.Mason.

Immediately W.H erected one of the most striking shop improvements ever seen in the High Street a façade of plate glass with a glazed, coloured earthenware surround. Inside was as impressive with all "the modern adjuncts of such an establishment". Equally impressive was the show of Christmas meat from Newport market made up of prize-winning animals from the Duke of Sutherland, Colonel Cotes and others.

John Mason was born here as was his father Frederick Roberts Mason the name coming from Lord Roberts the hero of the Boer War. But by March 1994 he had had enough, the landmark butchers shop was closed after nearly 100 years of trading in the High Street. The collapse of Tuckers, the ugly boarded up mess, the effect of having no pavement for two years which meant there was no passing trade, the problems with Wrekin District Council over payment for repairs to the building all added to the difficulties which arose anyway with the arrival in that era of the supermarkets. All butchers were going to struggle without the addition of special effects. Added to this were burglaries encouraged by the state of the building which meant higher insurance rates. The shop was, he said, becoming an expensive charity and though he felt sad for his staff and loyal customers there was no point in continuing. "We did not have to shut it but our trade had disappeared, and then Safeway opened and that was the final straw."

The lives of the Masons were blighted by streams of officials and the legal problems involving court cases in Birmingham, the judge, John maintaining, being the only one throughout the dispute, with any common sense. John could not cope with the enquiries and the business and left it to Liz who every night made a précis or diary of what had happened during the day. The great worry and tension affected their married life and perhaps over the years the diary, or the "buggeration file" as it came to be known, was a way of relieving this pressure. The collection of paperwork resulting from the long-running legal disputes eventually proved too large for the filing cabinet. The documents charted the various schemes put forward for the site, the six-year struggle to get their supporting wall repaired - for a time they could see the market hall clock through a gap in the kitchen wall - and the letters to and from councillors, officials and legal advisers.

As we have seen for the first year they were left with the living room and a kitchen with holes in the wall and the wedges falling out as the cracks widened. They moved out of Weston House in 1990 and went to live in "Le Paradoxie" in Beaumaris Road, taking the kitchen fittings with them! Having left the business and the building in 1994 they found it impossible to do anything with it. Eventually the insurance was paid to repair 51 High Street but the £84,000 was given to the developers who gave it to relieve the mortgage, the Masons got nothing. They invested in flats and for a time had students in them but they had to leave because of council regulations. They tried renting to an Irish Bar and then a bookmakers but planning was refused the Masons believing that the council did not want certain businesses at 51 which might conflict with their plans for 53 and 55. Having the key to the site allowed them to know what was going on – or not going on – but increased their stress. But in 2000 as the new buildings arose from the wreckage they were optimistic, "We always think everything turns out for the best so we're waiting for it. We hope it will." With the sale of Weston House in 2002 the cloud was lifted.

John and Liz Mason protest

The developers and their associates had folded their tents and left; the town had acquired new facilities, perhaps not to every ones taste, also a huge bill, while Liz and John Mason had endured years of distress. And then of course there was Mr Barnes the innocent passer-by on that lovely August morning.

When The Chickens
Came Home To Roost.

Newport has been familiar with the Irish problem for centuries the result of building the town on a road which was the main highway to that country, and down which politicians and soldiers marched to subjugate its wild people. Even after Telford built the A5 through Wales to Holyhead troops, guns and horses could still be found bivouacked overnight in Newport Square coming or going from Ireland. It was not one way, for generations Irishmen came down the now A41 for seasonal work on the farms of Cheshire and North Shropshire, welcome support for a labour intensive industry. In the industrial revolution they flocked into the cotton industry around Manchester contributing to low wages and poor living conditions. The potato famine in Ireland in 1845 and the years after reduced the population from 8 to 4 million, most died, many went to the United States to become policemen and presidents but many others surged into England arriving in Newport where the 1851 census finds them crowded, 13-14 to a house, in Cock Yard, Bellmans Yard and Marsh Lane. They were hawkers, pedlars, farm labourers, charwomen, excavators, poor and very young.

Highways carry not only goods they carry ideas and cultures and when mixed with drink they could make an Irishman quite volatile. There were frequent brawls in the High Street when hot summer nights brought them from their crowded homes and yards.   As we have seen there were serious riots in 1855 at the White Lion an Irish pub in Bellmans Yard and in 1857 at the Fox and Duck what was described as "a desperate and bloodthirsty struggle." There was fighting between the Irish and Donnington colliers, never reluctant to avoid a quarrel. Of course many moved on but many are still here with their own church and school.

The Irish "problem" continued and spilled over into mainland Britain. Violence and extremism were never far away though names may have changed.   Irish Nationalists gave way to the Fenians, who blew up people, then Sinn Fein, the Irish Republican Brotherhood then, as they split, the IRA, the Provisionals and on the other side the Loyalists. By 1970 the British Army was in Ulster fighting both sides. Internment was followed by "Bloody Sunday" when the 1st Battalion of the Parachute Regiment shot thirteen civilians. Less than a month later the officers` mess of the Parachute Regiment at Aldershot was bombed killing five women workers and a catholic padre. A pattern was being established that was to affect Newport.

In November 1987 as a crowd gathered at Enniskilen's war memorial a bomb went off killing eleven people and injuring 63. The timing and the place added to the revulsion but nothing changed, in fact it increased as Loyalists began to kill as many as the IRA and the Provisionals. In 1989 the recreation centre of the Royal Marines School of Music at Deal was destroyed killing eleven young bandsmen. In April 1992 there was a huge explosion in the commercial heart of the City of London destroying the Baltic Exchange and the Commercial Union's headquarters amongst other buildings. Three people were killed and the damage was estimated at £800 million the equivalent of all the compensation for bombing paid out in the previous twenty three years. This was the violent climate when the troubles came to Newport in 1989.

Tern Hill is on the A41 between Newport and Market Drayton in Shropshire. An RAF station it had become an army base named as The Clive Barracks and in November 1989 it housed the 2nd Battalion of the Parachute Regiment who were about to leave in a few days time. Early on the Tuesday morning of 21 February 1989 sentry Private Alan Norris, described by the newspapers as "steely eyed", disturbed several men at one of the residential blocks designed to hold 150 men though only about a third were there. His gun was deliberately empty and he had to load before he could fire three rounds. The terrorists escaped but after about twenty minutes three bombs exploded and devastated the sleeping quarters and injured one soldier with flying glass. The L shaped building had a gaping seventy-five foot hole and lots of rubble caused by an estimated 100lbs of Semtex. Five fire engines and forty firemen took over three hours to deal with the incident. Meanwhile a suspicious holdall on the car park was exploded.

Police tried to make links with two suspects from a bomb factory in London where detectives the previous year had found 200lbs of explosives and also with a find of explosives in Yorkshire.

The attack had been preceded by other incidents close by involving civilians. Brian Fleet of Rosehill Nurseries had disturbed a gunman on his premises at 3am that morning and thinking it was a burglar had told him to clear off. The lock of the door had been shot off and the bullet was later recovered. Tern Hill brick dealer, Arthur Simpson, had also come face-to-face with an armed, masked man that morning who demanded the keys to his car. It was also thought that one of the bombers had tried to flag down a car on the A41.

The bombers left their car in Woodridge Close a small residential area in Edgmond just down the road from Harper Adam's Agricultural College leading the police to believe that they were still in the area. Sixty of the Colleges 1060 students came from Northern Ireland or the Irish Republic and all were closely interviewed by the police. At the time of the attack one student, Kevin O'Donnell, was living in a hall of residence but he convinced the police that he had nothing to do with the bombing.

The police warned all hotels, pubs and boarding houses in the vicinity and questioned the landlady of the Lamb in Edgmond, Mrs Margaret Hazel, and her bar staff particularly about a group of Irish rugby students who had been playing the college. They also questioned the staff at the Pheasant in Newport a popular students' venue. A false alarm at the Pheasant turned out to be a visiting reporter on his way to Northern Ireland.

Residents were duly alarmed. At Edgmond police were criticised for taking a long time to evacuate Woodridge Close, while at Tern Hill there were questions about the security at the base.

Soon afterwards Mrs Thatcher, the Prime Minister, visited the college and O'Donnell again evaded the security checks on the students. Known as Barry to his fellow students he cultivated a reputation as a quietly spoken, hard-working student and was so successful that some of his fellow students even nicknamed him the "bomber" as a joke, being the last sort of person they believed who could be involved in terrorism.

On 22 May 1990 Kevin O'Donnell, still studying poultry husbandry at Harper Adams College was arrested in north London as a suspected IRA terrorist sparking off another major search in the Newport district when it was learned that he had been living at Wilbrighton Hall on the Aqualate estate just outside Newport on the Stafford Road. The Hall on a high ridge in Staffordshire, the watershed of the Trent and Severn catchment areas, had ceased farming in the hope of becoming a golf complex. When this was refused it reverted to accommodation for students, isolated, yet near the college, it gave a clear view of the surrounding area.

Recently restored Wilbrighton Hall

After his arrest on gun charges and given the Tern Hill bombings the police launched a search of the Hall for an arms cache. Tradition has it that this was in a hiding place alongside the former Stafford-Wellington railway line and right in view of O'Donnell from his room in the Hall. The straight road from Wilbrighton Hall to the A518 is crossed by a large embankment and a bridge for the Stafford railway. At the base of the bridge were two hydraulic rams supplied with water from a nearby pool and it was the empty chambers for these former rams that were thought to have provided the hiding place for the weapons. The continued thumping of these rams when they were in use gave the local name of the "Knocker Bridge" for this railway arch.

Police also hoped it would throw new light on the attack on the Clive barracks. Inspector Terry Lowe said students at the college were being interviewed, "Tern Hill is uppermost in our minds at the moment" he said. "We are making certain inquiries at Harper Adams College on behalf of the anti-terrorist squad. The enquiries encompass Tern Hill - we have got our eye on it." Given that the getaway car had been abandoned in Edgmond police renewed their suspicions that the IRA team could have been staying in the area.

Knocker Bridge

A fellow student raised the alarm when he recognised O'Donnell's picture on national television. Mrs Selina Juhre who owned the Aqualate estate and therefore Wilbrighton, was woken from her bed at midnight on the Tuesday as the police sealed off all approaches to the house. "O'Donnell had been there about a month, he came with a bunch of other students" she said, adding "As soon as I saw the police I said that's the man I met up the drive."

Other local residents said they had seen a column of police cars and armoured vehicles moving towards the hall on the Wednesday morning and two helicopters spent the whole day crisscrossing the area.

Det. Chief Superintendent Malcolm Bevington of Staffordshire police - Wilbrighton is just in Stafford - said police had closed the road off and had uncovered a number of items in the hall. "We have taken possession of a few things, it depends how the work is completed as to whether they become interesting", he said. The work was being done on behalf of the anti-terrorist squad to help with the O'Donnell case but also because of the proximity of Tern Hill. The police digging continued as did the interviewing of staff and students at Harper Adams.

Eighteen months later people were still nervous a Newport man sparking an alert and a huge search when he found a sheaf of suspicious IRA documents in the glove compartment in a car he had just bought. The fear was genuine particularly among publicans one landlady from the New Inn, having been advised by the brewery not to let anyone use the telephone in the back room - there were no mobiles then – as they might be IRA terrorists, refused such a request from a regular customer. A row ensued, the customer resenting being compared to a terrorist, resulting in him being banned from the public house several of his friends following him!

The college warden, Ian Robson, described O'Donnell as an average student, very quiet, not brilliant but one who had not failed his exams. He expressed astonishment at his arrest which had taken place after a high speed car chase in the early hours of Tuesday morning in north London in May 1990. He was charged with the illegal possession of two Romanian AKM 7.62 semi-automatic rifles and ammunition with intent to endanger life. These powerful Kalashnikov's were the IRA's favourite sniping rifle. Traces of explosives including a Semtex component were also found on his clothing and in his Ford Cortina car. He was remanded in custody for a week.

Detectives thought he had been caught red-handed but he refused to answer questions and told the jury at his trial that he been horrified to discover the weapons in his car which had been left with a cousin in London where it must have been used by the IRA to store them.

"The Irish Emigrant" reported his eight day trial at the Old Bailey where he pleaded that the rifles were there without his knowledge and consent. He was found not guilty but banned by the Home Office from the mainland. Within a few weeks back in Ulster he had been re-arrested after a loaded gun and a RPG-7 rocket propelled grenade were found in his car. His family maintained he was the victim of a police vendetta. These charges were also dropped when he said he was leaving to live in America.

There was a general feeling that the "baddies" were getting away with it again, "The Birmingham Six", six Irishmen who had spent sixteen years in prison after being wrongfully convicted for the 1974 Birmingham pub bombings, having been recently released. Alan Clark, a Conservative Minister, complained about the O'Donnell case that a jury would not even convict an IRA gunrunner who had "Kalashnikovs in the car and hands smelling of Semtex."

On the 16 February 1992 Kevin O'Donnell aged 21 a catholic in the IRA was killed by undercover British Army members in the car park of St Patrick's Roman Catholic Church, Dernagh, near Coalisland shortly after he had been involved in a machine gun attack on the British Army and RUC base in Coalisland, County Tyrone. Eight men led by O'Donnell took just one minute over the attack in which there were no casualties before going to the church car park where they were dismantling the machine gun ready to make their escape. O'Donnell and three other terrorists were killed in a burst of 580 rounds in fifteen seconds, and two others were wounded and captured and two escaped. Sinn Fein claimed the SAS and other British Army units had long used a shoot to kill policy naming in 1992 not just O'Donnell but Patrick Vincent, Sean O'Farrell and Peter Clancy.

O'Donnell even receives acknowledgement in the official history of Harper Adams College on the grounds that such publicity, although not sought, kept the college before the public eye. He did arouse some sympathy in the public being killed without warning, the newspapers emphasising his charmed life, his daring and luck in fooling the college, the police and a jury and because he was named Kevin Barry after a famous martyr and hero of Irish ballads. Certainly his lecturers and fellow students expressed shock at his sudden death and the secret life of the Gaelic-speaking, likeable, quiet, charming young man.

On the 25 August 1992 the IRA planted three fire bombs in Shrewsbury, in Shoplatch, The Charles Darwin Centre and Shrewsbury Castle, the latter causing the most damage as the castle housed the Shropshire Regimental Museum and many priceless historical artefacts were lost and damaged by fire though there were no injuries or fatalities.

It is arguable that O'Donnell was sent as a "sleeper" to the college by the IRA to be activated when required to take arms and explosives to the active units. Was he actively involved at the Tern Hill barracks or the supplier? Did he play a key role in the IRA campaign on the mainland? Evidence after his return to Ireland shows he was very involved and he was given an IRA funeral.

The sectarian violence did not end despite declarations and the decommissioning of weapons. The IRA destroyed the offices of the Ulster Defence Association over a fish and chip shop in the Shankill Road in 1993 killing nine people including two girls aged seven and nine. During the next eight days the loyalists retaliated with fourteen killings. In December 1993 they blew up the London Docklands at a cost of £85 million and in August 1998 twenty nine lost their lives through a bomb in Omagh. 3,600 people had been killed up to 2002 the British army having lost 700 and the RUC more than 280. People had reason to be alarmed even in small country towns like Newport, Shropshire.

One man Robert Hendy-Freegard callously exploited this fear. If there is no connection between him and Kevin O'Donnell there ought to be as the one nurtured the other.

At Blackfriars Crown Court on 6 September 2005 Sarah Smith, John Atkinson and Maria Hendy turned to each other and gripped hands. They had just seen Robert Hendy-Freegard jailed for life which meant he would stay behind bars until at least March 2013. A bizarre story which began in 1992 in a pub in a scared Newport ended at Terminal 4 of Heathrow airport in May 2002, ten years later. Bizarre enough to become a television documentary called "The Spy Who Stole My Life" produced for Channel 5 on 7 September 2005.

Robert Freegard was born on 1 March 1971 in Hodthorpe a small village near Whitwell in Derbyshire not far from Worksop, Nottinghamshire. Described as "semi-literate" he left school at 15 with no qualifications was on a YTS scheme, worked for a construction company and took a City and Guilds course in carpentry which later made him the butt of jokes such as did he work for MFI or MI5? In 1993 he was convicted at Nottingham Crown Court on two charges of theft involving £1,500 from a girlfriend. Other charges of kidnap were left on file. He adopted the name "Hendy" along with other disguises.

In 1992 he was working as a part-time barman in the ancient "Swan" public house in Lower Bar, Newport, having followed the young lady to the town with whom he had had a relationship and from whom he had borrowed money. Here he met three students from Harper Adams College which is located in the nearby village of Edgmond and who lodged a few doors away from the pub. It was the custom, and still is, for students to seek refreshment and entertainment in the town of Newport particularly on Wednesdays, which is the student recreation day, and Fridays. The three were Sarah Smith, from Kent, Maria Hendy, from Somerset, whose name he took, and John Atkinson, from Cumbria.

This was the time of the death of Kevin O`Donnell and it would be difficult to believe that these three did not know the background to this case including the connection with Harper Adams College. Hendy allegedly told John Atkinson that he was a Special Branch officer, MI5, Scotland Yard or other variations, and that his job as a barman was a cover for his investigation of an IRA cell at the college. Pursuing this line he persuaded John Atkinson to help with the "mission" and subjected him to beatings in the cellar of the pub to ensure that he was hard enough for the task. He also convinced him to behave oddly around the college to prove his loyalty and to alienate him from his friends. Freegard was very keen on "loyalty tests" which bound his victims - sometimes literally - ever closer to himself.

Despite these precautions Freegard revealed that their cover had been blown by the IRA, and that they were in danger of elimination not just by the IRA but also by the security services. They had to escape and take the two girls with them. At first he told the women that Atkinson had cancer and persuaded them to give all their money and leave on a "farewell tour" for Atkinson. They arrived in Sheffield and it was only at this point that Freegard told the women of the IRA threat and told them to sever all outside connections because of the danger to their lives. The saga leaves Newport and assumes another dimension. For Atkinson in meant giving up his university finals, handing over £300,000 and going on the run from imaginary republican assassins for three years. During this time he carried out a series of weird missions, spurious jobs and "training" for Freegard, having to wait for days in places for non-existent meetings convinced that "my country needed me". At last he told his sister the IRA was after him and the tale began to emerge.

Others became entangled such as farmer William Atkinson who through his son John was swindled out of his life savings, over £390,000, under various pretexts including starting up a plumbing business and protecting John from the IRA. William would hand over the money to John's girlfriend, Sarah Smith, at motorway service stations and shopping centres being told terrorists were amongst the shoppers watching their every move. It was not until after four years, 1997, that Mr Atkinson finally realised they were being conned and John Atkinson was able to break free. He became an English teacher in Prague. "He ruined my life. It was degrading and humiliating. They were very serious things that he was lying about, you do not joke about the IRA."

As for Sarah Smith, Freegard was charged with her kidnapping and the theft of £210,000 including loans from her mother for £23,000 and £23,500 as well as £99,000 from a trust fund. She was described as the longest suffering victim for over ten years. When the group split up in Sheffield she was only allowed to keep her tips from work. Her father Peter, a wealthy farmer from Canterbury, employed private detectives to no avail to bring his daughter home and suffered death threats, not knowing whether she was dead or alive. He was suspicious at once when Sarah just six weeks before the end of her three year degree course at Harper Adams, left with her boy friend John Atkinson. She said she had got a "super job" and could not be persuaded to complete the course. She asked for money in May 1993 to buy a car and when this was refused Mr Smith was verbally abused over the telephone and threatened with death by John Atkinson and Freegard's mother Roberta. More demands came from Sarah and he handed over £99,000. Sarah Smith gave evidence in court as to how she had been ferried to a so-called safe house with a bucket over her head and had hidden in cupboards to avoid visitors, once spending three weeks in a locked bathroom with little to eat, convinced she would be shot by a sniper. Years later she still found it impossible to make choices or decisions, "...the bars Freegard created in my mind" she said, "trapped me as surely as any physical restraint".

Maria Hendy became his lover giving birth to his two daughters. When she eventually found out about his other affairs she was beaten, threatened and forbidden to talk to anyone for security reasons. She spent eight years with him mostly in a cramped flat in Sheffield.

Freegard went on to deceive and defraud Caroline Cowper, Elizabeth Richardson, Renata Kister, Simon Young, Leslie Gardner and Kim Adams and it was her mother who lured him to his arrest at Heathrow, Kim still believing it was part of a police "test".

Peace came to Ireland eventually but given the location of Newport in those violent days, given the incidents at Shrewsbury Castle, Tern Hill and other IRA attacks at Milford near Stafford and Whittington station near Lichfield, given Kevin O'Donnell and Robert Hendy-Freegard, it is not difficult to believe that Newport was the centre of some sinister cell, that in a quiet, remote country town there was an unpleasant, frightening terrorist presence.

In April 2007 at the Court of Appeal, Freegard had his conviction for kidnapping quashed the Judges ruling that his victims had not technically been kidnapped. All that he was left to serve was a nine year sentence for fraud and theft which meant that he could be released by November 2007. Two months later, Sarah Smith the Harper Adams student who met Hendy-Freegard towards the end of her course, wrote a book of her experiences appropriately called "Deceived: a true story".

Footnote.

Like the Greek maidens who attended the sacred flame in the temple of Olympus Marjorie Cooper keeps vigil over a beloved relic of the Cooper family - a shoe. But this is no ordinary shoe it was worn at the battle of Trafalgar in 1805 and stood next to Admiral Nelson as he lay dying on HMS Victory.

Extract from The Death of Nelson by Daniel Maclise (1806-70)
John Cooper appears front right of centre.

If you visit the Royal Naval Museum in Portsmouth you can actually ask to see the shoe which is kept in the reserve collection and then walk across to the Victory on which the shoe served. The leather shoe was donated to the museum in 1955. Its wearer had been John Cooper who served as a "landsman" on the Victory and for his part in the battle was awarded £4.12.06 (£4.62) and £1.17.06 (£1.87) in prize money.

These were the years of the French Revolution and Napoleon Bonaparte when Europe disappeared and many in England rolled up their maps of the Continent believing they would never be needed again. Add to this the Industrial Revolution and the Agricultural Revolution these were very turbulent times and there was a need for heroes and John Cooper was on the front line with Nelson and the Duke of Wellington.

John was born in 1772 and as a young man was pressed into the army but preferred the navy and as soon as it was possible he deserted his regiment and sought active service at sea. Given the insatiable need for men the navy took him in without question and he soon saw a great deal of fighting on the Bellerophen, a former French ship, in the Mediterranean. In one of these engagements his right leg was shot away and for a long time he lay in hospital. When he recovered he was fitted with a wooden leg and without hesitation rejoined the navy serving as a cook, a familiar allocation in that period for men with such disabilities. They were labelled "landsmen" on the muster roll but in the heat of battle served the guns and suffered the blacking of the powder smoke, the noise and the mayhem of the gun decks. Wooden ships manned by wooden legs.

He served at Ushant and on the "Ganges" at the battle of Copenhagen in April 1801 which prevented the Danish fleet falling into the hands of Napoleon. It was at this battle that Nelson put his telescope to his blind eye and claimed he could see no ships. On the 16 May 1803 John sailed with Nelson on the Victory in the Mediterranean and then followed the cat and mouse game with the French fleet across the Atlantic before Nelson cornered the Franco-Spanish fleet of 33 ships under Villeneuve off Cape Trafalgar on its way from Cadiz to Naples. The French lost 20 ships the English none, the greatest loss being the death of Nelson.

John was serving the guns on the Victory and received a bonus and prize money but his greatest award many years later was to feature in the large painting by Daniel Maclise (1806-70) of the death of Nelson which hung in the Royal Gallery at the House of Lords and now in Liverpool Museum. This is a wholly imaginary, inaccurate though heroic portrayal as Nelson died deep in the bowels of the ship, below the water line safe from the guns not on the top deck. Nevertheless John is there the second figure on the right of the Admiral, tending the wounded, his wooden leg clearly visible.

Our sailor John survived which is why he appears in the picture being one of the last crew members available and remained in the navy until 1826 when he retired after 36 years service on an enhanced pension. His naval record shows him as a Greenwich out pensioner in 1829 aged 48 after serving 23 years 11 months with a life pension of £29.20 having sustained a fractured thigh. The difference in age and dates between different accounts is explained by the fact that the lower decks were often illiterate or uncertain of the facts about themselves and would give different answers on different occasions. The fractured thigh would be the original injury which necessitated amputation.

John made his home in Knutsford and married three times. He died in 1859 at the reputed age of 87 and was buried in Knutsford church. The 1841 census has him aged 65, a navy pensioner with wife "Pheeby" aged 35. In 1851 he is described as born in Knutsford aged 76 a Greenwich pensioner with Phoebe and her son from a previous marriage. They had five children the youngest 8 years old.

Sailor John had a grandson William John Cooper, born 1860, who became a master baker and as a young man in 1884 moved from Cheshire to the market town of Newport, Shropshire and opened a business in Upper Bar. By 1885 he had married a Wellington girl and had a young daughter. Having prospered, in September 1901 he moved across the road to 25 Upper Bar installing new steam ovens and a double shop front. He advertised as a grocer, tea dealer and confectioner, baker, flour and provision merchant with homemade pork pies a speciality. William John was a noted sportsman particularly bowls and football. He was a founder member (1904) of the Newport Bowling Club winning many awards and exhibiting them in his shop window along with photographs of himself. He was a keen official of the football club. Like his grandfather Sailor John, he was sociable, cheerful with a generous disposition.

William John needed all these qualities in 1916 when his two younger sons were killed fighting in France defending their country from a continental enemy just like their great-grandfather Sailor John had done a hundred years earlier.

The shoe makes a remarkable footnote to Newport history.

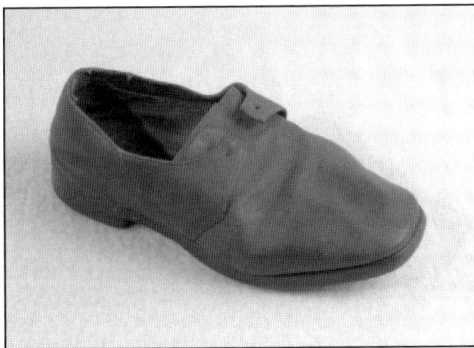

John Cooper's Shoe

Courtesy of Richard Noyce
Curator of Artefacts
National Museum
of the Royal Navy

HOME MADE PORK PIES A SPECIALITY.

COOPER

WILLIAM J. COOPER,
Grocer, Tea Dealer & Confectioner,
BAKER, FLOUR & PROVISION MERCHANT,
THE STEAM BAKERY,
UPPER BAR. NEWPORT.
SALOP.

Sources:

What Happened to the Vet. Newport Advertiser (NA) July and September 1858. Thanks to Mrs M.J.Ray, Reigate, Surrey, great granddaughter of Frederick Arthy. Census returns Colchester and Newport. Directories.

The Adams Family. NA 1889 to 1907. Also Williams, Heather, "The Lure of the Land", Harper Adams, 2000, chapter one. Picken Papers, in the possession of the author.

The Irish. Census returns 1841-1901. NA 1858, 1882, 1916, 1939 etc. Donnelly, James S., "The Great Irish Potato famine", Sutton Publishing 2001. Thompson, Flora., "Lark Rise to Candleford" p234ff. Coleman, Terry, "The Railway Navvies", Penguin Books, 1965. Trinder, Barrie, "The Industrial Revolution in Shropshire", Phillimore, 1973. Log Books, SS Peter and Paul, School, Newport. Personal reminiscences Vincent C McDonald, Rockville, Maryland. Newport: Martin Moran, John Kelly and Bill Kane. Barbara Spellman Shuta, Irene Walsh Nunnari and Lynn Gay descendants of Michael Kilcoyn in the USA.

The Sudden and Furyous Fire. Transactions Shropshire Archaeological Society IX p163-170; TSAS X p118. Parish Register. Miles, M.F., "History of Newport Market Company", 1993. NA from 1854, particularly August 1870, June 1874, November 1910. Miles M.F., "Newport's War" 2004. Picken Papers. Minutes of Local Board 1875. UDC minutes from 1894. History of Hinstock. Torr, Cecil., "Small Talk at Wreyland", OUP, 1979. "Advertiser Almanack", Bennion, Horne and Smallman, 1899.

Duchess Blair: NA 3 December 1892, 24 December 1892, 3 June 1893 and 3 August 1912. Stuart, Denis, "Millicent Duchess of Sutherland 1876-1955", Victor Gollancz, London, 1982. Magnus, Phillip, "King Edward the Seventh", Penguin Books, 1964. Keppel quote from James Lees-Milne "Beneath a Waning Moon", John Murray, 2003, p 193.

A Funeral and Four Weddings. Wheat, Mable, "Chetwynd", 1954. Davies, Elizabeth R, "The Rylands", 1996, Archives NDHS. Liddle & Heane Collection, Shropshire Archives. Robertson, D.H., "The Sleepy Meese", 1988. Ruscoe, Anthony, "Landed Estates and The Gentry", Vol.4, 2000. Watson-Jones, Peter, "Chetwynd Parish Church", 1998.

NA 22 November 1890, 3 September 1898, 5 July 1902, 14 August 1909, 1 June 1912, 11 January 1913.

The Marked Man. NA 1892-1904. School log books for the period. Daily Graphic 21 May 1896.

Milliners Tale. NA 13 November 1902, 2 April 1904, 22 January 1910. Mate, C.H., "Shropshire Biographical", 1906.

The End of the Gentry. Miles, M.F., "Newport People", 2004. Juhre, Ted, "Aqualate Family Connections", 2005.

Town Versus Gown. NA 1929. School affidavits in private ownership. Times Educational Supplement, 1929. Also, Taylor R and D, "Mr Adams' Free Grammar School", Phillimore, 2002. p139/40.

The Newport Shootings. NA March 1943.

Hey-Ho Come To The Fair. Newport & Market Drayton Advertiser. Miles, M,F., "Newport (Shropshire) Trading and Market Company", 1993. Freda Allen and Ned Williams, "Pat Collins King of Showmen", Uralia Press, 1991.

Where Has What Was Ours All Gone? Based on newspaper reports and Health Authority reports of the time. Pugh, Martin, "We Danced All Night", Vintage Books, 2009. p55/56.

It All Fell Down. NA and Shropshire Star (SS) archives from 1989. Many thanks to Liz and John Mason for discussing the events and consulting their original notes.

When The Chickens Came Home to Roost. NA and SS for the years concerned. Williams, Heather, "The Lure of The Land", 2000. p276. Clark, Alan, "The Last Diaries", Weidenfield and Nicolson, 2000. Smith, Sarah, "Deceived", Orion Publishing, 2007.

Footnote. Most of the information comes from the collection of Mrs. M. Cooper of Newport, a descendant of John Cooper. Other information and photograph of the shoe is courtesy of Richard Noyce, Curator of Artefacts, National Museum of the Royal Navy.